The superb gold of an Ogon

Other titles in this series:

The Tropical Aquarium
Community Fishes
Coldwater Fishes
Marine Fishes
The Healthy Aquarium
Garden Ponds
Aquarium Plants
Central American Cichlids
Fish Breeding
African and Asian Catfishes
South American Catfishes
Livebearing Fishes
Fancy Goldfishes
African Cichlids

AN INTERPET GUIDE TO

KOI

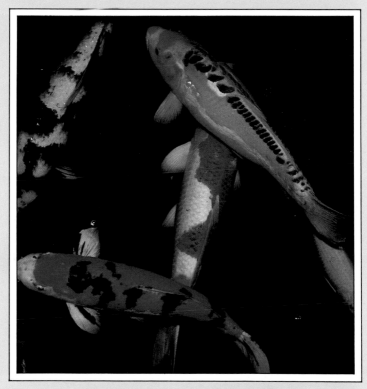

Brilliant Koi reflecting the colours of the Orient

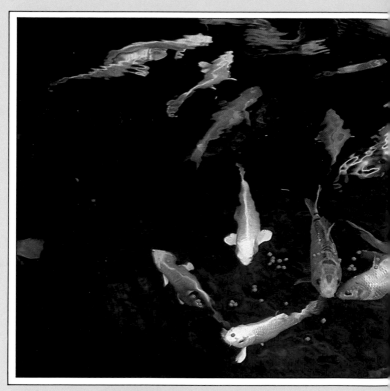

Young Koi feeding on floating pellets

AN INTERPET GUIDE TO

KOI

Comprehensive advice on maintaining and displaying
these spectacular ornamental carp

Barry James

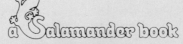

a Salamander book

Published by Salamander Books Limited
LONDON • NEW YORK

A Salamander Book

A corner pond suitable for small Koi

Credits

Editor: Geoff Rogers   Design: Roger Hyde
Colour reproductions:
York House, Melbourne Graphics Ltd.
Filmset: SX Composing Ltd.
Printed in Belgium by Henri Proost & Cie, Turnhout.

Author

An early obsession with the natural world led Barry James to pursue botanical and zoological studies at London University. Using his wide experience of the commercial aquatic world, he opened his own aquatic nurseries some 16 years ago. His main interests include oriental water gardening. He contributes regularly to the aquatic press, both as an author and photographer, and acts as a consultant worldwide to planning authorities, corporate bodies and private individuals on aquatic matters, including conservation projects.

Consultant

Glyn Evans is a Director of one of the leading specialist Koi companies in the UK. He regularly travels to Japan to select Koi for the Kent-based business and is a recognized Judge and Member of the Japanese Nishikigoi Dealers Association. Having studied fluid dynamics as a ship designer, he spends much of his time designing and developing new filtration and Koi pond systems.

Contents

Introduction 10

Basic anatomy 12

Pond construction 14

Filters, pumps and aeration 22

Water gardens 34

Buying Koi 44

Feeding 48

Seasonal care 52

Diseases and predators 56

Breeding and showing 70

Koi varieties 74
A photographic survey of popular colour
varieties presented simply in terms of
one, two, three and multicoloured forms

Index 114

Picture credits 117

Introduction

The Common Goldfish – smaller and without barbels.

Nishikigoi, or Koi, are the national fish of Japan. 'Nishiki' is the Japanese word used to describe a highly coloured cloth. 'Goior Koi' is the Japanese name for carp. Together, therefore, 'Nishikigoi' means 'coloured carp'.

Iran is thought to be the ancestral home of the Common Carp (*Cyprinus carpio*), from which Koi were first developed. This wild carp, which is an excellent food, was carried to Japan, China and Western Europe by traders about a thousand years ago.

Koi were first bred in Japan in the 1820s, initially in the town of Ojiya, in the Niigata prefecture. Carp were used for food and were stored for eating during the winter. These brown fish produced occasional red and blue mutations, and selective breeding of these mutants resulted in the development of new varieties. By 1870, the Kohaku (red on white) variety was perfected. Many of the other currently recognized varieties were developed by the 1930s and new ones are being established all the time. In Europe, a mutation arose with only a few large glossy scales. This so-called Mirror Carp was sent from Germany to Japan, where it was crossbred to

produce varieties known as Doitsu-Goi, or German Carp.

Koi differ from Goldfish in their origins. Goldfish (*Carassius auratus*) share a common ancestry with the Crucian Carp (*Carassius carassius*) and were developed in China, where carp have been bred for at least 2000 years. They do not grow as large as Koi, and the two species can be clearly distinguished by the fact that Koi have two pairs of barbels on the upper lip, while Goldfish have none.

Koi-keeping is an immensely popular hobby in Japan, and Koi clubs hold many exhibitions and shows, with lavish prizes for the winners. The stakes can be high, with prize-winning fish changing hands for enormous sums of money.

Since the Second World War, Japan has exported many thousands of Koi to the West. Enthusiasts in North America and Western Europe have not only imported stock for sale, but have started fish farms in order to breed their own Koi. Koi are also bred in Israel and Singapore. So far, the fish produced have not matched the quality of those from Japan, but as knowledge of the techniques increases, no doubt the standard will improve.

Basic anatomy

The basic external appearance of a Koi is similar to that of other bony fishes. It has an elongated body, but is stocky with a high back. The mouth is directed forward and its fleshy lips are protrusible. There are two pairs of barbels on the upper lip.

Fins
Koi have the normal array of fins for propulsion and manoeuvrability. The single tail, or caudal fin, propels the fish forward, but also acts as a rudder for changing direction. The single dorsal fin along the back acts as a stabilizer, keeping the fish upright and preventing it rolling. It has three or four hard rays followed by 17-22 soft rays. The anal fin also has a stabilizing function. It has three hard rays followed by five branched soft rays. The paired pelvic, or ventral, fins located approximately midway along the lower body are used for directional change; each has two hard rays and eight or nine soft ones. The paired pectoral fins near the gill covers are also used for changing direction; each has one hard ray and 15 or 16 soft rays.

Gills
The gills, which are protected by stiff gill covers, or opercula, consist of a number of filaments containing a fine network of blood capillaries. The arteries and veins feeding and draining these capillaries run directly from the gills to the heart. Water continually passes over the gills, the flow being caused by the pressure difference created by the fish opening and closing its mouth. Since the gills present a large surface area to the water flow, the blood capillaries take up oxygen from the water and release excess carbon dioxide produced by the normal processes of respiration. Thus, the gills are equivalent to the lungs of land-based animals. Since the gills are extremely vulnerable to damage and infection by parasites or disease organisms, it is vital to keep a close check on their condition. (See also Diseases and predators, pages 56-69.)

Senses
Koi have keen eyesight, but the eyes are very vulnerable to injury since they lack the protection offered by lids. As in most fishes, the nostrils in Koi act as the organs of smell. This very important sense is mainly used for locating food and is backed up by the 'taste' receptors in the barbels around the mouth. As foraging fishes, Koi rely heavily on

External features of Koi

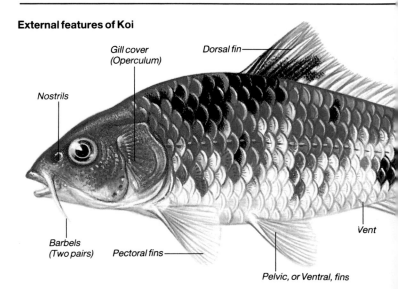

Gill cover (Operculum)

Dorsal fin

Nostrils

Barbels (Two pairs)

Pectoral fins

Pelvic, or Ventral, fins

Vent

these 'sensitive antennae' to distinguish suitable food from other detritus in the water and in the substrate.

Although Koi can certainly hear, they rely more on the so-called lateral line system to detect and pinpoint sound waves and pressure changes under water. The lateral line system is literally a line of pressure receptors located in 35-39 closely arranged holes running along the flanks of the fish. Nerves connect these receptors to the spinal cord and brain.

Internal organs
The jaws are not equipped with teeth, but teeth do occur further back as outgrowths of the pharynx. These sift tiny organisms from the water. The short oesophagus leads directly to the intestine; Koi do not have a stomach. In adult fishes, the intestines may be up to 3.6m (12 feet) in length, and they produce digestive fluids rather like those in the stomach of higher animals.

The functions of the liver and pancreas are carried out by one organ, whereas the gall bladder and spleen are separate. The rectum, ureter (from the bladder) and sex organs all have their outlets at the vent, located in front of the anal fin.

Skin, scales and colour
The basic body consists of three layers; mucus on the outside; scales (when present); and skin. It is essential for the health of the fish that these layers remain undamaged, since they act as 'lines of defence' against the entry of disease-causing organisms. The scales in Koi, unlike those of the original wild carp, can be very variable in size and shape due to the influence of the large-scaled Mirror Carp and the effects of selective breeding. In some types, for example, the scales are relatively small and in others absent altogether.

As with other fishes, variation in the colour and patterning of Koi is caused both by the amount and position of reflective guanin in the skin and by the presence of true pigments. The many colours and patterns of Koi are recognized internationally by their Japanese names. Although at first difficult to grasp, these names are built up logically from simple terms that denote colour, pattern, resemblance to natural forms, and also reference to the periods of history in which they were developed. The different Koi varieties available and the names used to describe them are featured in Part Two of the book, beginning on page 74.

Size and life expectancy
In ideal conditions in Japan, Koi have grown more than 95cm (37.5in) in length. It is quite possible for Koi to reach 70cm (27.5in) in good conditions in Europe or America. Life expectancy varies widely depending on individual circumstances; 'Hanako', the oldest Koi in Japan, was reputed to have lived for more than 200 years. Kept in the correct environmental conditions, it is possible for Koi to achieve a lifespan of 60 years.

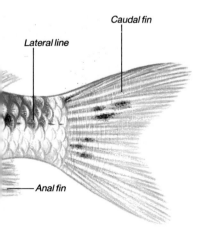

Caudal fin

Lateral line

Anal fin

Left: *Although beautifully patterned and bred in a wide range of colours, Koi are basically carp, with all the anatomical features typical of that family of bony fishes.*

Pond construction

Constructing a pool for keeping Koi is no longer the chore that it was several years ago, when concrete was virtually the only material available. Koi-keepers can now choose between several lightweight materials, including fibreglass, PVC and butyl rubber, all of which can be installed quickly and easily. Even the excavation of the hole need not be the backbreaking job it used to be. Mini-excavators are now available for hire at reasonable cost and these can be used to dig out even quite large holes. These machines will pass through a gap of only 75cm (30in) and so can gain access to even the smallest sites.

Siting the pool

Since water accumulates naturally at the base of slopes and in valleys, your Koi pond will look most natural at the lowest point of the garden.

Above: *A small informal pool built at two levels using a high-quality PVC liner, with Golden Orfe in the lower level and Koi in the upper level.*

Take care, however, that it does not become a 'sump' for waterborne pollutants. Position the pond in a clear unobstructed spot that receives plenty of sunlight, although some shade at midday is beneficial to protect Koi from strong ultraviolet rays during the summer. Sunlight will not only ensure that the water absorbs heat to maintain the fishes' metabolism at the right level, but will also encourage water plants to flourish (see page 42). Avoid large trees; falling leaves will pollute the water in the autumn and aphids will drop down and infect the water plants. Also be sure to provide shelter from any cold prevailing winds; hedges or slatted fences are ideal because they 'filter' the air flow without the fierce turbulence that occurs on the leeward side of brick walls or other solid barriers.

In Japan, Koi pools are traditionally situated near to the house. The pool may come right up to the walls or may even go beneath the foundations so that it reappears in the living room! The owners can then enjoy their fish all year round. Electrical and water supplies are also easier to provide if the pool is near the house. If it can be situated close to a drain then water changes and cleaning are easier too.

Below: *A large formal Koi pool built in concrete. It is heated in the winter and uses both biological and sand pressure filtration systems.*

Pool design
Pools may be formal or informal in design. In general terms, if your garden is laid out on geometrical lines, then a formal design, such as rectangular, square, circular or L-shaped, will look better. However, the tendency today is towards informality in the garden; Japanese gardens are invariably informal. As most pools are made with flexible liners, oval and kidney shapes are the most popular because they make the most economical use of a rectangular sheet of liner, and they also result in fewer creases.

Whatever shape of pool you choose, bear in mind that the minimum depth should be 1.2-1.5m (4-5ft). This will allow sufficient unfrozen water for the fishes to survive during the winter in severe climates. (See also pages 54-5.)

Pond construction materials

There are three basic types of material for constructing a Koi pond: concrete, flexible liner and fibreglass. Here we review the pluses and minuses of each type and offer installation guidelines.

Using concrete

Once the only choice available, concrete is now the least attractive option for building a garden pond. Even highly engineered and professionally built concrete ponds are liable to develop flaws and leak at some stage. All materials naturally containing water or having water added to them during the building process, such as bricks, blocks, concrete, mortar and rendering, will shrink as the water evaporates. The cracking that results is often hastened by the 'freeze and thaw' action that occurs during frosty weather. It can be very difficult, therefore, to keep a concrete pond waterproof.

If you are determined to build a concrete pond, the following points may be helpful:

● Prepare the ground well and ensure that the base of the hole is firm and level.
● Allow for a wall thickness of at least 15cm (6in) for a large pond.
● Use a dry mix of one part suitable grade cement, two parts of clean sharp sand, three parts of coarse ballast, and the manufacturer's recommended quantity of waterproofing powder.
● Slowly add water until a stiff consistency is achieved. Use a cement mixer for large quantities.
● Position bottom drains, overflow pipes or connecting pipes from water pumps before you concrete.
● To construct the sides of a formal design of pond, position a sturdy framework of timber panels with spacers so that it is 15cm (6in) away from the excavated sides.
● Incorporate any reinforcing materials, such as steel rods or

Above: *The first of three views of a professionally built Koi pond. Here, the filters in relation to the pond.*

ESTIMATING POND VOLUME

It is important to know the volume of water in your pond, particularly to set stocking levels, to choose the correct size of filters and for the effective dosing of the pond with chemicals such as disease remedies and algicides. Here, we offer simple formulae for estimating water volume in litres, Imperial gallons and US gallons.

Regular shapes
Litres (Measure in metres)
Length × width × average depth × 1000 = volume in litres.
Imperial gallons (Measure in feet)
Length × width × average depth × 6.24 = volume in Imperial gallons.
US gallons (Measure in feet)
Length × width × average depth × 7.5 = volume in US gallons.

Circular pools
Litres (Measure in metres)
Radius squared × average depth × 3.14 (π) × 1000 = volume in litres.
Imperial gallons (Measure in feet)
Radius squared × average depth × 3.14 (π) × 6.24 = volume in Imperial gallons.
US gallons (Measure in feet)
Radius squared × average depth × 3.14 (π) × 7.5 = volume in US gallons.

To measure the water volume more accurately, which may be the only way for complex shapes, fit a flowmeter into the pipe used to fill the pool. Alternatively, divide up your pond into simple shapes and calculate each one separately.

mesh, before pouring in the wet concrete. Remove air by tamping down or vibrating the concrete.
● Remove the shuttering when the concrete is hardened but before it is completely set.
● Avoid having sheer vertical sides; the pressure of ice forming in the winter will crack the walls. Slightly sloping walls will allow ice to ride up.
● Leave the surface of the concrete layer rough so that the finishing coat adheres well. Use a rendering mix of one part suitable grade cement, three parts of clean sharp sand plus

the waterproofing powder.
● Complete the rendering coat in one go and smooth it with a trowel.
● Cover the pond with damp sacking or newspaper; spray this regularly with cold water during hot weather to prevent cracking.
● Leave for at least a week for the concrete to harden completely.
● Apply a very generous coat of non-toxic proprietary pond paint to the rendered surface in order to build up a thick bed of elastic material that will bridge any cracks that do develop in the surface.

Left: *Ample size – 6m(20ft) long and 1.8m(6ft) deep. Fibreglass covers the concrete rendered surface.*

Above: *Wooden decking hides the three-chamber filter system and provides a striking garden feature.*

Flexible liners

These are, without doubt, excellent materials for pond construction. The choice available includes polythene, PVC (with or without nylon reinforcement) and butyl rubber sheeting. The latter – supplied in black and about 0.75mm (0.03in) thick – is the most expensive but, with a guaranteed life of more than 20 years, it is easily the most suitable material. Long-lasting liners made from ethylene propylene (EPDM) and blends of butyl rubber and EPDM are also available. Take care choosing EPDM liners, however, since some EPDM is manufactured with the use of 'oil fillers' that can contaminate the pond water and kill the Koi.

Once you have decided on the size of your pool, use the following simple formula to calculate the size of sheet required. Take the length plus twice the maximum depth for the first dimension, and width plus twice the maximum depth for the second. For instance, a pool measuring 3.6x3x1.5m (12x10x5ft) would need a liner mesuring 6.6x6m (approximately 22x20ft). If you want to make absolutely sure of having sufficient overlap around the edge for finishing, add a further 60cm

Below: A typical 'pond plumbing' set-up, with an economy bottom drain connected via a token length of 10cm(4in) pipe to a standpipe.

(24in) to both dimensions. Liners can be tailor-made at the factory so that they fit snugly in rectangular pools without creasing. As this involves extra seaming and cutting, there is a small extra charge for this service.

Here, we review the basic steps in installing a liner. Remember that bottom drains and other pipework must be put in before installation of the liner.

1 Measure out on the ground the longest measurement of the pool and put in a couple of pegs as markers. Now do the same with the width. Take a length of rope or hosepipe and run this around the pegs to make the shape you require.
2 It is a good idea to install a concrete collar approximately 30cm

Enlist help to ensure that the liner is correctly located in the hole as you add water. Allow a generous 'safety margin' around the edge for neat finishing.

A layer of sharp sand provides a smooth surface for the liner and cushions it against punctures from jagged stones.

Seal the liner between edging stones and collar

Edging stones

From bottom drain to discharge box

(12in) wide and 15-23cm (6-9in) deep at a depth of about 30cm (12in) below ground level. This will help to maintain the finished shape and reduce crumbling during excavation.
3 Start digging from the centre outwards, removing soil as you go.
4 When you come to the sides of the pool, dig the walls at a slight angle to prevent them from crumbling, which happens with loose soil if the sides are dug vertically.
5 When the excavation is finished, use a spirit level and a long straight edge to check that the top is level.
6 Remove any jagged stones and put in a layer of sharp sand. Although you can use newspapers or old carpet to cushion the liner, consider laying some of the fluffy synthetic matting designed for this.
7 You will need the help of at least one other person to install the liner, although if a total of four people are available, so much the better. First unroll the sheet and spread it over the hole. One person should now get in with bare feet to push the liner into position while the others tug the liner to smooth out creases and to make sure that there is an even overlap all the way around the edge.
8 Now start to fill the pool using a hosepipe. Station all helpers at equal distances around the pool and give small tugs to the liner to straighten out any creases. Remember that even 5cm (2in) of water across the base of the liner weighs an enormous amount. Continue this until the pool is full.
9 Trim the edges of the liner and secure it with paving slabs or stones to your own requirements.

Installing a liner pond

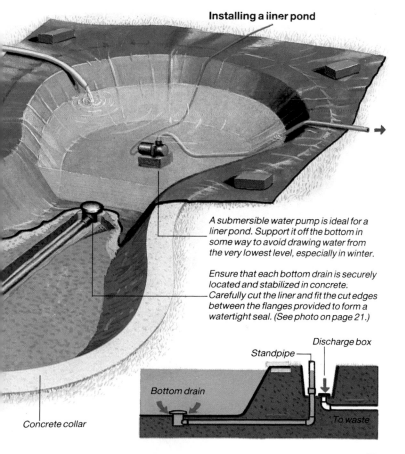

A submersible water pump is ideal for a liner pond. Support it off the bottom in some way to avoid drawing water from the very lowest level, especially in winter.

Ensure that each bottom drain is securely located and stabilized in concrete. Carefully cut the liner and fit the cut edges between the flanges provided to form a watertight seal. (See photo on page 21.)

Discharge box
Standpipe
Bottom drain
To waste
Concrete collar

Fibreglass ponds

Pre-formed fibreglass 'shells' are available in a variety of shapes and sizes, most of which are too shallow for Koi. However, specialist manufacturers now produce more spacious models with depths of 1.2-1.5m (4-5ft).

Install a fibreglass shell as follows and be sure to fit bottom drains and other pipework at the same time.

1 Place the shell upside down on the ground and mark with a spade around the edge, drawing its outline on the ground.
2 Dig the corresponding hole a little deeper than the actual pond depth, to allow space for a layer of sharp

sand about 10cm (4in) thick.
3 Place the base of the pond on the sand layer; this will protect it from stones in the subsoil. Check that the pool is level.
4 Begin infilling around the sides of the pool with the subsoil. Use a hosepipe to wash down the soil so that no empty spaces are left.
5 Place the topsoil around the edge. You may need to add more soil after a few days to allow for settlement.
6 Finish off by laying and cementing paving or rockwork around the edge.

Fibreglass can be applied in situ to any shape of excavation. Basically, the task consists of applying a resin (mixed with a precise amount of

Installing a fibreglass pond

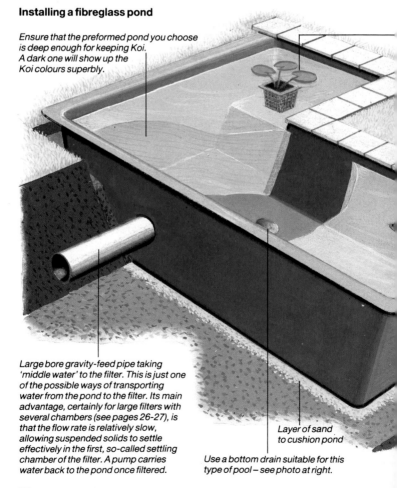

Ensure that the preformed pond you choose is deep enough for keeping Koi. A dark one will show up the Koi colours superbly.

Large bore gravity-feed pipe taking 'middle water' to the filter. This is just one of the possible ways of transporting water from the pond to the filter. Its main advantage, certainly for large filters with several chambers (see pages 26-27), is that the flow rate is relatively slow, allowing suspended solids to settle effectively in the first, so-called settling chamber of the filter. A pump carries water back to the pond once filtered.

Layer of sand to cushion pond

Use a bottom drain suitable for this type of pool – see photo at right.

hardener) to a layer of glassfibre matting. At least two layers are needed. Well done, this technique can produce a very good result. If doing it yourself does not appeal to you, professional pond companies can apply the glassfibre layer.

Bottom drains

As an integral part of pond construction, you should consider installing at least one bottom drain. These are designed so that small fish cannot escape when the pool is being drained. They are available as ready-made units and should be installed at the deepest part of the pool. Two basic types are available: one for use with liners, which has a double flange to form a tight seal around the cut edge of the liner; and a version for use with concrete and fibreglass pools, which has a single flange that can be simply rendered in place. The drain is normally attached to a 10cm (4in) diameter PVC pipe which leads to a brick-built discharge box at the side of the pool. The water is released through a valve or standpipe to a drainage system or soakaway.

If you are adapting a pool which does not have a bottom drain, there are models which can be fitted at the top of the pool. These are connected to a pipe that siphons the debris from the bottom, and are known as 'top-bottom' drains.

Water lilies, properly planted in baskets, are among the few aquatic plants that will survive the attentions of the Koi. The marginal shelves in a preformed pond shell are ideal locations for such plants.

Once you have filled the gap between the shell and the edge of the excavation with subsoil (and some sand, if necessary), use suitable stones to cover the exposed edge of the casting. For a stable and attractive finish, bed these on mortar.

Ideally, set the pipe from the pond bottom drain in concrete.

Above: *A bottom drain suitable for use with a liner. The cut edge is trapped between the two flanges.*

Above: *A bottom drain for concrete or fibreglass pools. A seal is created with rendering or fibreglass layers.*

Filters, pumps and aeration systems

A pond ecosystem can be self-sustaining if it is well stocked with plants, has a balanced number of fishes and receives adequate sunlight. However, the persistent 'rooting' habit of Koi allows few plants to survive, and thus to maintain good water quality the Koi-keeper will need to install a filter, pump and aeration system. In this section, we look at the different filter types available and then consider the installation of suitable pump and aeration systems in a Koi pond.

Filtration processes
Filtration is the process by which debris is removed from the water, while at the same time organic waste products are converted into less harmful substances. There are three basic methods of filtration: mechanical, chemical, and biological. Often more than one of these methods is in operation at the same time in any particular filter system.

Mechanical filtration This is simply the mechanical removal of solid detritus as the water passes through a suitable medium, such as gravel, sponge or synthetic fibres. The trapped solids are then removed from the system, either by back-flushing into a drain or by taking out the filter material for cleaning or replacement.

Chemical filtration In this case the filter medium exerts a chemical influence on the water as it passes through. Commonly used chemical filter media include zeolite and activated carbon, which will extract organic wastes, inorganic chemicals and carbon dioxide from the water.

Biological filtration As the name implies, this method of filtration makes use of natural biological processes to purify the water. Although they vary in design, all biological filters support a colony of aerobic bacteria (i.e. those that flourish in oxygen-rich conditions) that convert toxic ammonia produced by the decomposition of

organic wastes into progressively less harmful substances that are then recycled in the so-called 'nitrogen cycle'.

The principal so-called nitrifying bacteria involved are *Nitrobacter* sp., which convert ammonia (NH_3) to nitrites (NO_2), and *Nitrosomonas* sp., which convert nitrites to nitrates (NO_3). In a well-balanced system, the nitrates are absorbed by growing plants as a fertilizer and the plant protein then becomes a food source for the animals within the pond, thus completing the cycle.

Filter media
Before we look at the working principles of various filters, we review the common filter media and their characteristics.

Processed lava granules The sponge-like formation of these granules gives them a high surface area-to-volume ratio: they are covered with crevices on the outside and have a matrix of capillaries on the inside. Because of its structure, this material is a very efficient physical filter. It also encourages biological filtration because it provides a large surface on which beneficial bacterial colonies can form. It is inert, sterile, neutral in pH and very light, with a dry density of about $500kg/m^3$ (approximately $40lbs/ft^3$).

Baked clay granules These lightweight spherical granules are favoured by many filter manufacturers. They are also used for hydroculture, i.e. growing plants in a fertilized solution with the granules acting as an inert support.

Gravel This is available in several grades; the coarser grades of about 6mm (0.25in) particle size are probably the best. Canterbury Spar is a much favoured gravel medium because the irregular shape and porous nature of the particles provide a large surface area as a haven for beneficial bacteria, as well as producing good mechanical straining properties. A particle size of 6-10mm (0.25-0.4in) is ideal.

Sand This can only be used in sand pressure filters, because it clogs quickly and needs frequent back-flushing – a difficult procedure with many gravity-fed filters. (See under 'Sand pressure filters', (page 30.)

Foam Foam can act as both a mechanical and biological filter, but it has a tendency to clog and therefore needs frequent cleaning. There are many types of sheet foam, but be sure to avoid those which have been treated with fire-retardants or those in which cyanide is used in their manufacture as these types can be poisonous to fish.

Plastic mouldings These are becoming very popular because of their enormous surface area. They range from plastic shapes used in the biochemical industry, such as tubular pieces of UPVC, to household items, such as hair rollers, which are much cheaper and just as good.

Filter brushes A Japanese idea that has gained favour for both mechanical and biological filtration is to pass the water through a series of long-bristled brushes. The bristles sieve out a great deal of suspended solid material and provide a generous surface area on which nitrifying bacteria can thrive. Cleaning is simply a matter of opening the drain cock and gently shaking the rods that support the rows of filter brushes.

Zeolite This is a chemical filter medium which removes nitrites and ammonia from the water. It comes in the form of off-white or light-brown chippings of various sizes, and is made of hydrated silicates of calcium and aluminium, sometimes with sodium and potassium. Keep it in a container that can be easily removed for recharging. Do this by soaking the chippings overnight in a concentrated salt solution. After rinsing and drying, they are ready for further use in the filter system.

Below: *Various filter media.*
1 Filter brush, effective as both a mechanical and biological filter.
2 Commercially produced plastic mouldings. 3 Canterbury Spar gravel. 4 Large grade zeolite.
5 Baked clay granules. 6 Small grade zeolite chippings. 7 The effect of malachite green on zeolite.
8 Processed lava. 9 Freeze-dried bacteria to 'seed' biological filters.

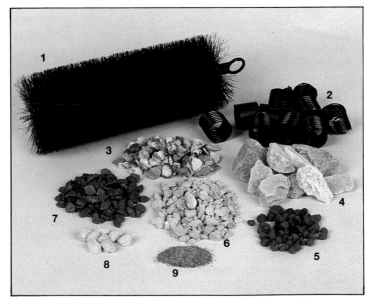

Filter designs

There is a wide range of filters on the market. These cater for everyone, from the beginner with a small pond to the specialist with a large pool full of many valuable fishes.

Multipurpose filters Basic designs consist of a large plastic container equipped with standard plumbing fittings. The water is pumped up to them from the pond and it then flows up or down, depending on the design, through a filter medium held in one main chamber. This type of filter is quite unsightly and so needs to be disguised in some way. You can let it into the ground provided that the outflow pipe is above the pond water level, or you can keep it above ground and disguise it as a wellhead by constructing a stone wall around it. Pre-filters are available that fit on to the inflow of the pump. These trap larger particles of debris before they reach the main filter, thereby prolonging its life and overcoming the need for frequent back-flushing.

Above: *A single-chamber filter with six rows of filter brushes, plus zeolite granules in the exit port.*

Upflow filter

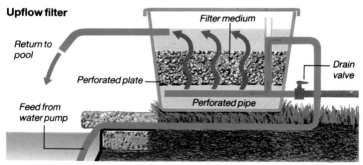

Return to pool

Filter medium

Drain valve

Perforated plate

Perforated pipe

Feed from water pump

Above: *A stylized upflow filter in action. A variety of filter media can be used in the single chamber, typically Canterbury Spar gravel.*

Below: *In the summer, when the water is warm and the fish active, position the pump further from the filter to create currents in the water.*

Summer set-up

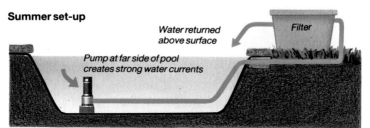

Water returned above surface

Filter

Pump at far side of pool creates strong water currents

Left: *A submersible pump that could be used to supply the filter systems shown on these pages.*

Above: *A basic filter chamber fitted with filter brushes being used to maintain Koi at an exhibition.*

Downflow filter

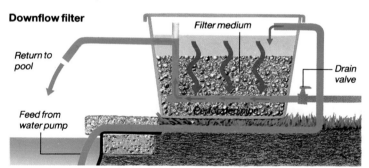

Filter medium

Return to pool

Drain valve

Feed from water pump

Perforated pipe

Above: *The working principles of a simple downflow filter. A perforated pipe buried in the filter medium carries water back to the pond.*

Below: *In the winter, position the pump further off the bottom and closer to the filter, and return the water to the pond more 'smoothly'.*

Winter set-up

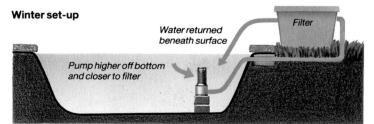

Filter

Water returned beneath surface

Pump higher off bottom and closer to filter

Larger filtration systems for the specialist with very big pools consist of several chambers. The first one will be a settlement chamber where large debris falls to the bottom and may be siphoned out or removed by a drain cock. The subsequent chambers operate on an over-and-under system, each one containing a different medium to carry out a specialized cleaning function. The second chamber will contain a coarse filtering medium, such as filter brushes, then the next chamber could contain Canterbury Spar and the final one, zeolite – as shown on this page.

In most cases, these multichamber filters are gravity fed by a large-bore pipe (10-25cm/4-10in in diameter) and the water is returned to the pond by a pump in the final filter chamber. This method is used to reduce the velocity into the filter to a minimum and thus allow maximum settlement of suspended solids from the inflowing water.

These types of filters hold very large volumes of water, but this is necessary in relation to the total volume of the pond. Commercial models can be very expensive, although it is quite possible to make your own from basic components.

Right: *Installing a multichamber filter system. The large bore gravity feed pipe to the first chamber can be seen at bottom right. The discharge box is at the extreme left.*

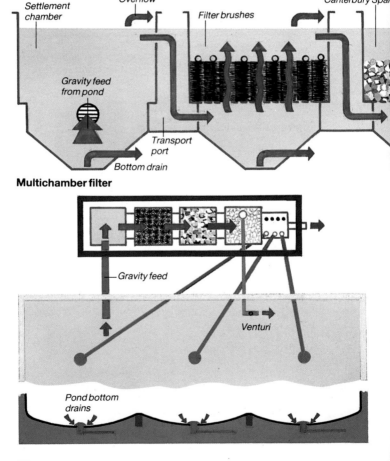

Multichamber filter

26

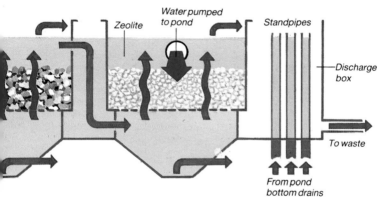

Zeolite

Water pumped to pond

Standpipes

Discharge box

To waste

From pond bottom drains

Left: *A plan view showing how the above filter could relate to a Koi pond. Each of the three areas of the pond can be drained individually. Below: A side view showing the gravity feed pipe from the pond to the settlement chamber of the filter.*

Above: *A typical multichamber filter system in action. Each chamber has a separate bottom drain for cleaning purposes, and a system of valves allows pond water to bypass certain chambers – when treating the water with disease remedies, for example.*

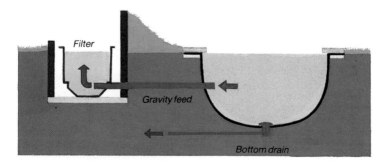

Filter

Gravity feed

Bottom drain

Undergravel filter This type of biological filter is essentially a larger version of the system used in aquariums. The aim is identical in both cases: to set up a constant water flow through a bed of gravel at the bottom of the aquarium/pond in which aerobic nitrifying bacteria can flourish to purify the water as it passes through. Since the design and size of Koi ponds varies so widely, you will need to construct the necessary pipework from basic components. Use PVC pipes of 37mm (1.5in) bore and build up a suitable framework using 'T' pieces, elbows and cross-pieces to cover at least one third of the pond's floor area. Drill 6mm (0.25in) diameter holes at intervals along the tubes, spacing these about 20cm (8in) apart on the tubes near the outflow pump connection and lessening the distance between them down to about 10cm (4in) in the 'outlying' areas of the grid. This will help to set up an even water flow over the entire area of the filter. Drill the holes in pairs at an angle of 45° from the bottom of the grid, as shown in the illustration.

Place a plastic mesh with 12mm (0.5in) perforations over the

framework of pipes – this will prevent clogging – and build up a brick enclosure around the edges. Add a layer of gravel (1cm/0.4in particle size) to a depth of 20-30cm (8-12in) over the grid and connect the system to a submerged or external water pump. When turned on, the pump will draw water downwards through the gravel, into the pipes and then back to the pond through the outlet side of the pump.

Left to itself, and with the pump running, the gravel bed will develop a thriving colony of aerobic bacteria over a period of several weeks. This maturation period depends on the temperature of the water and on the presence of suitable organic wastes to 'seed' the process. To speed matters up, it is possible to add sachets of freeze-dried bacteria that in ideal conditions will 'mature' the gravel bed in seven to ten days.

Since the bacteria need a constant flow of oxygen-rich water to thrive, it is essential to keep the pump running continuously. If it is switched off for any length of time, the colonies of aerobic bacteria in the gravel will die, often with dire results for the fish since the dead bacteria release toxins.

Undergravel filter

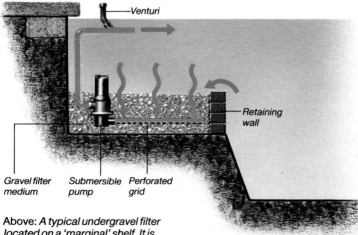

Gravel filter medium · Submersible pump · Perforated grid · Venturi · Retaining wall

Above: *A typical undergravel filter located on a 'marginal' shelf. It is important to keep the water flowing through the gravel bed to maintain the aerobic bacteria that perform the biological cleaning action.*

Right: *A cutaway of the filter shows how the gridwork of pipes draws in water from the entire gravel bed.*

Above: *The submersible pump shown on page 24, fitted with an undergravel adaptor. The moulding* *replaces the original base plate and allows the connection of a pipe to carry water from the pipe gridwork.*

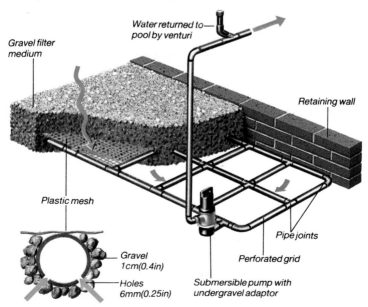

Water returned to pool by venturi

Gravel filter medium

Retaining wall

Plastic mesh

Gravel 1cm(0.4in)

Holes 6mm(0.25in)

Pipe joints

Perforated grid

Submersible pump with undergravel adaptor

29

Vegetable filter

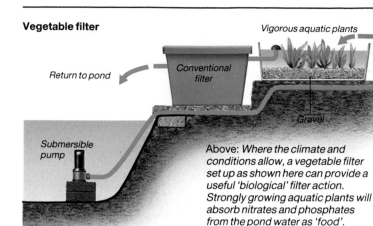

Vigorous aquatic plants

Return to pond

Conventional filter

Gravel

Submersible pump

Above: *Where the climate and conditions allow, a vegetable filter set up as shown here can provide a useful 'biological' filter action. Strongly growing aquatic plants will absorb nitrates and phosphates from the pond water as 'food'.*

Vegetable filter This is basically another type of biological filter, but filled with growing plants rather than a bacteria-rich medium; Japanese and Chinese fish-breeders, in particular, use this system. For a Koi pond, it simply involves setting up a second pond or container at a higher level planted with vigorous aquatic plants, such as *Sagittaria* sp. (Arrowhead), *Eichhornia crassipes* (Water Hyacinth) and, only in warm climates, *Pistia stratiotes* (Water Lettuce). These aquatic plants are greedy feeders and will absorb nitrates and phosphates from the pond water pumped into the container. An overflow pipe from this 'vegetable filter' can direct the water to a more conventional filter system on its way back to the main pond. The only maintenance required is to thin out the plants periodically, thereby removing the salts at the same time (i.e. incorporated in plant tissue). Naturally, this system will work more effectively, and over a longer period, in warmer rather than cold climates.

Sand pressure filters These are more popularly associated with swimming pools, but they are also used in Koi ponds. However, they are usually used as a supplement to biological filters, the sand acting as an efficient mechanical filter to any suspended solids still in the water. Because they can be back-flushed easily, they do not clog up as often as other models which use

diatomaceous earth as the filter medium. Various sizes are available.

General filter requirements Whether you are buying a filter or creating your own system, there are certain factors to be taken into consideration, particularly for filters with a biological action.

Surface area The surface area of the filter medium determines the number of bacteria that can colonize the system. This in turn dictates the rate at which ammonia and other toxic wastes are removed and, consequently, the health and growth rate of the Koi.

Volume of filter material The volume of filter material should not be less than 10-15 percent of the volume of the pond and, in any event, should not be less than $0.5m^3$ ($17.6ft^3$)

In the case of plastic filter media, the weight of fish that $1m^3$ ($35.3ft^3$) of filter medium is capable of supporting depends on the amount of ammonia produced in the pond. Normally $1m^3$ will support 75kg (165lb) of fish. This assumes that the recommended feeding schedule is followed, that the fish are a uniform size of 30-45cm (12-18in), and that the filter is sufficiently mature and well aerated.

Flow rate The flow of water through the filter must be 'in tune' with the filtration processes at work. If it is too powerful, for example, it will prevent the build up of a beneficial colony of bacteria by tending to dislodge them.

Oxygen concentration The water flowing over the filter medium must be well oxygenated. Tests carried out on the outflow from the filter should still reveal an appreciable level of oxygen in the water. (See 'Aeration systems', page 33.)

Turnover rate Selecting the right pump is very important, as the rate at which the pond water is recycled through the filter should be such that toxic levels of ammonia and related organic waste materials are not allowed to build up in the pond. As a guideline, all the water in the pond should pass through the filter in one to two hours.

Below: *A sand pressure filter. These units are available in various sizes. Be sure to match the pump size with filter capacity to achieve the most efficient flow rate. A 'multiport' valve controls water inflow and outflow, back-flushing and rinsing.*

Pumping systems
The principal function of a pump is to circulate water around the pond. This can include an ornamental feature, such as a fountain or waterfall, or simply set up a flow to and from an external filter. Remember that the pump merely circulates the water present in the pond; never connect a mains water supply directly to a waterfall or fountain, as the chlorine and other purification chemicals added to the water may kill the fishes.

There are two kinds of pumps: submersible and surface-mounted. The former are more popular because they are easier to install and maintain. The range of pumps is enormous and they vary in price according to their performance and robustness of construction. All are capable of running off standard mains voltage, although some models use a step-down transformer to reduce the voltage to a lower AC voltage or to a very low DC voltage.

Be sure to use waterproof connectors for all electrical fittings in the garden. As a safety

Sand pressure filter

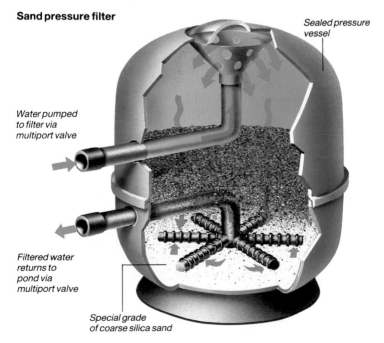

Sealed pressure vessel

Water pumped to filter via multiport valve

Filtered water returns to pond via multiport valve

Special grade of coarse silica sand

precaution, incorporate a circuit breaker in any mains circuits; this device will automatically cut off the power should there be any leakage of current. If you are in doubt, always consult a qualified electrician to install the system.

Study the literature carefully before buying your pump. The main factors to consider are:

Above: *A water pump that can be used either as a surface-mounted unit or fully submerged in the pond.*

Output What is the output in litres (or gallons) per hour at a standard 1m (3ft) head, and how does the performance fall away when you need to lift the water to higher levels? For instance, a pump may deliver 4550 litres (1000 gallons) per hour at a 1m (3ft) head, but only 1680 litres (370 gallons) per hour at a 3m (10ft) head. If you are using an external filter, does the volume of water delivered by the pump satisfy the manufacturer's requirements?

Electrical consumption What is the electrical consumption of the pump? For instance, two pumps may both deliver 1800 lph (400gph) at a 1m (3ft) head, but one may consume 90 watts of electricity, while the other uses 210 watts.

Pond draining When emptying the pond, can you use the pump to drain it right down to the bottom?

Fountain or waterfall Some pumps deliver a high volume at low pressure, which is fine for a waterfall, but unsuitable for a fountain, where relatively low volume at high pressure is needed.

Compatible fittings Each design of filter has fittings for certain diameters of hosepipe; does the pump take the size required?

Principle of the venturi
Below: *The principle of the venturi tube, named after the Italian physicist who devised it. A restriction in the pipe causes the water flow to accelerate and the resulting drop in pressure brings in air to create a turbulent air/water mixture. A simple way of regulating the amount of air is shown at right.*

Cap on air intake tube

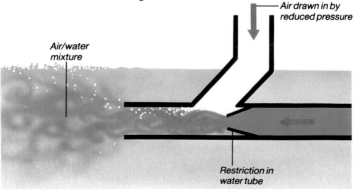

Air drawn in by reduced pressure

Air/water mixture

Restriction in water tube

Above: *Ready-built venturi tubes are available from Koi specialists in a range of sizes. Match the size with your pump capacity and flow rate.*

Aeration systems

Many systems are used to increase the oxygen concentration in the water. Most of them involve quite bulky structures, such as air-exposure towers, which are located outside the pond. However, a small submersible device successfully used in commercial fish farms is now available for domestic ponds. This is known as a mat aerator and it gives excellent results. Basically, it consists of a plastic or stainless steel cylinder which, for pond use, is available in diameters of 5-10cm (2-4in). Air is supplied to the unit by a blower operating at a pressure just sufficient to overcome the static head (pressure exerted by the water above it) and friction losses. The air is first delivered to a diffuser in the base of the unit. As it rises, the air acts as an air-lift pump, moving the mixture of diffused air and water upwards through the cylinder. Venturi rings (normally three) deflect the air and water mixture on to three free-turning turbines, the centre turbine rotating counter to the others. The combined effect is to shear the air bubbles into a froth of tiny bubbles, causing turbulence in the mixture and impeding the upward flow. The air/water interface is thus maximized, giving an extremely high oxygen saturation level. In addition, substantial aeration occurs in the surface boil caused by rising air bubbles.

Less complicated aeration devices can also be used. An aquarium air pump in a waterproof housing will supply a small amount of air, for example, and will work best fitted with a lime-wood airstone. The venturi is a popular system which can be made or bought. To make one, place a small restriction in the return pipe from the filter so that the passage is narrowed but not blocked. Bore a hole in the pipe just after the restriction and cement an airline pipe into position. As the water pushes past the restriction, it will create a partial vacuum which will draw air into the tube.

Water gardens

In this section, we look at Oriental and Western water gardening, past and present, for ideas which can be adapted to make an effective and appropriate setting for a Koi pond.

Western gardens are admired for their formal beauty. While this means that their layouts are generally based on traditional geometrical designs, they do vary considerably: each garden is very much the creation of the individual gardener. A Japanese garden, however – although just as much a personal expression of its maker – is designed to reflect the natural landscape of Japan. It represents in miniature the mountains, valleys, streams and shorelines which make up that country's breathtaking scenery.

In present-day Japan, land is scarce and only the wealthy have large gardens. Otherwise, these are only found in public parks and temple grounds. However, with amazing ingenuity, Japanese gardeners have created exquisite retreats from quite small town plots, reflecting the principles, if not the grandeur, of larger gardens. Outside the Orient, gardeners have incorporated many Japanese ideas into their water gardens, while still retaining the flowers and grass traditionally associated with Western gardens.

Oriental gardens

As early as the beginning of Christianity, Europeans were intrigued by the mysteries of the Orient. In the 13th century Marco Polo brought back fabulous tales of the palaces and gardens of China, and further reports about Chinese art and culture were sent back by Jesuit priests working in Peking. In Europe at that time, gardens were highly stylized, with geometrical shapes dominating the thinking of landscape architects. Chinese gardening, on the other hand, was essentially natural, with every facet designed to be a facsimile of the surrounding countryside. Like landscape painting, gardening in China was thought of as 'shan shui' (mountains and water) and was

closely linked to the other arts of poetry, calligraphy and sculpture. Chinese gardens were rarely seen all at once, but were meant to be discovered scene by scene as the observer strolled from one view to the next. Buildings such as temples, rest rooms and tea rooms harmonized with the environment, being built of natural materials such as bamboo and thatch. These buildings were sited in elevated positions to offer different views of the various features in the garden.

The Chinese and Koreans had such feeling for natural beauty that it is not surprising their near neighbours, the Japanese, were influenced by them. Japanese gardeners first adopted this basic style and then evolved their own, incorporating Shinto and Zen Buddhist teachings into their gardening philosophy.

Contemporary Japanese gardens are monochrome. Mosses, gravel, grasses, shrubs and trees, with their subtle and wide-ranging gradations

Above: *A Japanese public park with the simple harmony of colour and design typical of Oriental gardens.*

Below: *A bridge and waterside irises, Oriental garden features that can be incorporated in the West.*

of green, grey and silver, are all used to great effect. Trees are very important to the scene. They are mostly evergreen, although deciduous maples (*Acer* sp.) are also favoured for autumn colour. Pines and other trees are carefully clipped and trained with wires to give a gnarled weatherbeaten appearance. Pines, in particular, are revered as standing for silence, solitude and old age. Bamboo implies strength and pliability. Peach, plum and cherry trees in blossom herald spring and are held in high esteem. Evergreen azaleas and small-leaved box hedges are clipped and pruned into close rounded shapes to resemble rocks, turtles and tortoises. Irises are used at the edges of pools; otherwise flowers are generally only grown in the garden by 'vulgar and ignorant' people. Bonsai is, of course, another activity involving miniaturization, and Bonsai trees are used extensively in Oriental gardening schemes.

Features of Japanese water gardens

Ancient 'rules' give detailed instructions about the stones and other features of Japanese gardens, including gateways, bamboo fences, walls, pools, lanterns and stepping stones. Lanterns are elaborately classified. They are used at night to light the way for visitors to the tea houses, and to illuminate other garden features, such as bridges.

This use of lanterns is another extraordinary example of Japanese thinking: their gardens are designed to be seen in moonlight, at sunrise, at sunset and in frosty and snowy conditions. Gardens are also planned for the changing seasons, and vantage points are especially designed to enable cherry blossom to be seen at its best. Raked gravel and moss are used instead of grass. This is a positive design feature but also partly due to the severity of winter in many parts of Japan, where grass does not thrive.

Rockwork

The types of stones, their structure, features and correct placement are the most important elements in the design of a Japanese garden and water gardens. Stones which are waterworn are used in water gardens, while rugged rocks are used in mountain scenery. This extensive use of rockwork, often involves the use of huge boulders weighing several tons apiece.

Emulating such design features can cause problems; stone is expensive and even a small piece can weigh a substantial amount. Delivery, offloading and positioning (which often involves a mini-crane) will be charged as extras. But bear in mind that the amount of stone needed will only be proportionate to the size of the pool. If possible, stones should be waterworn. It is also better to use local stone wherever possible, as this will harmonize with the environment. However, the stone must be hard and durable. Remember that the same type of stone may vary greatly. Limestone, for instance, has

Above: *A European public garden created in the Japanese style, beautifully blending water features with a rich and varied planting.*

many forms. From some quarries the stone is hard and will last for years; from others the product is soft and crumbles after the first frost. So, for both aesthetic and economic reasons, local stone scores heavily over the imported variety.

Several types of stone can be used in a water garden. Here are some popular examples:

Limestone is hard and durable. Waterworn varieties are very popular. Colours range from off-white, through buff and grey, to deep red.

Sandstone varies in colour from yellow, through grey-pink, to reddish brown. Being a stratified rock, it is attractive in the garden.

Granite and other igneous and metamorphic rocks are very

durable. These are often well coloured and sometimes waterworn. Highly recommended.

Slate is stratified and can look very dramatic. Colours range from blue and green to purple.

Tuffa rock is a superb soft rock. It is very porous and soft, providing an ideal home for rockplants and ferns. It is very light in weight but it is relatively expensive.

Water

Japanese pools are normally informal and surrounded by large boulders set firmly in position. Flat areas are incorported to allow easy access for feeding and viewing. These are often paved with flat waterworn stones, with the edges kept in place by cedar logs set in a vertical position. Concrete mouldings of these logs are also frequently used. Trees and bushes are incorporated among the rocks, creating a cool refreshing atmosphere with an air of mystery. Streams are wide but shallow, the bed being filled with stones and boulders to make gushing and gurgling water sounds. The

Below: *An American University garden with well-positioned rockwork and stone ornaments that reflect the Oriental influence.*

37

reflective properties of water are greatly admired, so few aquatic plants such as water lilies and oxygenators are grown. This means that either the stream must be a natural one, or filters must be used to give crystal clear water.

Sand and gravel

The Japanese are fond of using sand or gravel both for pathways and to create special effects. Formerly, sand was used to prevent the feet getting muddy; in later years it was used to signify purity by the Zen masters who developed gardens based on philosophical themes. Sand in the garden today often represents a body of water, and rakes are used to create wave and ripple patterns to heighten the effect. The preferred type of sand has large grains, about 2mm (0.08in) in diameter, and is available in many colours. Mounds of earth or rocks, planted with moss and perhaps dwarf trees, are set amid the sand and gravel, to represent hills and mountains or rocky shorelines.

Stepping stones and pavements

Stepping stones are used both in the water, to enable the owner to cross the pool and so have a better view, and in the grass or moss gardens, to prevent the shoes becoming soiled in wet weather. Sometimes they have a symbolic significance and are carved with words, for example, to indicate the

Below: *A shishi odoshi, a traditional water-driven device originally intended to scare away wild deer.*

seven steps to heaven. Pavements are normally made of natural stone in a form of crazy paving. They are often kept wet by regular spraying to bring out the full beauty of the stone's texture and colour.

Stone ornaments

Stone ornaments traditionally featured in Japanese gardens include lanterns, towers, buddhas and signposts; they are intended to indicate the presence of humanity. By providing light for orientation, directions, or a place in which to worship, they help to make the garden a part of daily life.

Tsukubai and shishi odoshi

Tsukubai are basins containing water for hand washing. These were used before the tea ceremony. A bamboo cup on a long handle and a couple of bamboo sticks for it to rest on are necessary accoutrements.

Shishi odoshi are 'devices' originally developed by farmers for scaring away wild deer and to prevent them from eating the crops. Water is fed through a hollow bamboo pipe into an angled length of thick bamboo. This is set on an axle and has a hollow first joint. Water drips into this cavity, its weight forces the front tip of the bamboo downwards, and the water is released. The pole springs back up and the rear end strikes a small rock carefully positioned behind it, making a sharp, clacking sound. Shishi odoshi are often used at the edge of pools, sometimes as the source of a stream or waterfall.

Streams, waterfalls and bridges

Streams and waterfalls are carefully designed, many types being recognized according to the pattern of water flow they produce. By varying the design, a variety of sounds and visual effects can be produced. Bridges are a popular feature and can be quite elaborate highly-painted wooden structures or simple planks, slabs of stone or curved concrete artifacts. Often, bridges are combined with stepping stones, enabling visitors to cross the pool in several places.

Above: *Carefully positioned stepping stones lead the eye and the foot to a tea house strategically positioned in the subtle depths of a Japanese-style garden. Such ideas give creative food for thought.*

39

Bamboo fences and gates

The fence is an essential part of the Japanese garden. It ensures privacy and prevents the outside world from intruding. There are many traditional designs in various materials.

Plants for the Japanese garden

We have already mentioned the reasons for using certain plants and trees. Here are tips for growing them successfully.

Bamboo This is a giant grass and certain species grow to enormous proportions in the tropics. In cool temperate countries, however, you will find the hardy, spreading types. Bamboos are evergreen, but can shrivel in winter if they are not given adequate protection from the wind. Plant them on a sun-facing slope if possible, and make sure they are watered and fertilized regularly. Keep them in check by periodically pruning the rhizomes, which tend to stray out of the area designated for them. Propagate them by division.

One of the taller species of bamboo suitable for gardens, *Arundinaria simonii*, spreads quickly by underground runners and can reach a height of 5.5-6m (18-20ft). The leaves may reach a length of 30cm (12in) and a width of 38mm (1.5in). A dwarf species very popular in Japan is *Arundinaria (Sasa) veitchii*. It prefers shade and grows about 1m (39in) tall. It has a yellow stripe running down the edges of the leaves. Excellent for moist soils.

Moss This will grow well in shady moist areas and is commonly used as a ground cover in Japanese gardens. Many species can be collected in woods, but ideally choose the cushion-forming types. Moss gardens must be watered every day in the warmer months if possible. If you wish it to grow on rocks, chop the stems up finely and mix them in buttermilk. Paint the mixture on to the rock face and keep it well watered until it is established.

Azaleas These will only grow in acid to neutral soils – the presence of lime is death to these plants. Plant

Above: *A corner of a Japanese-style garden combining the harmonious sound of falling water with the visual delight of bright azaleas set against a muted background of principally green plants. Waterfalls, classified by design into many categories, are an important theme in Oriental gardening and can form an integral part of a landscaped Koi pond.*

Right: *A show garden incorporating the formal geometry of a gravel bed with the unique artistry of a Bonsai tree positioned to maximum effect.*

them in an ericaceous compost and clip them in late summer after the flowers have faded.

Box The Japanese favour this rather dull shrub because of its ability to tolerate hard pruning. Box (*Buxus* sp.) is an accommodating plant that tolerates lime well; it is thus an ideal substitute for azaleas in chalk or limestone areas.

Pines This group of trees will grow in the poorest soils. The gnarled twisted appearance is achieved by clipping and training.

Bonsai These truly delightful miniaturized trees are freely available in the West, although the prices are somewhat high. It is possible of course to train your own Bonsai and there are plenty of good books available with full instructions on the techniques required.

Western water gardens
Water gardening in the Western hemisphere has developed only over the last few hundred years. It shows a greater diversity than the water gardens found in Japan. The Dutch, French, Italians and the British, for example, have all developed their own styles. The Italians were influenced by Roman and Greek landscape architecture, so their water gardens are mostly very formal, with geometrical shapes and fountains rather than waterfalls. The British borrowed from other styles but have also developed a style of their own. Their water gardens are normally informal, incorporating rock- and bog-gardens, with waterfalls rather than fountains. The British are great plant and flower lovers, so pools tend to be heavily planted with water lilies and other deep marginal plants. They also use many submerged oxygenating plants as well as floating plants. The edges are generally heavily planted with marginals and bog and moisture-loving plants.

For Koi pools, however, planting aquatics is a problem because of the persistent rooting habits of the fish. Oxygenators are quickly uprooted, floating plants are eaten, and the soil from the containers is strewn around the pool, causing an unsightly mess! However, it is still possible to have colour and greenery in a Koi pond, provided that the plants are selected and planted with care.

Water lilies Water lilies – all species or hybrids of *Nymphaea* – are suitable for Koi ponds. Select the most vigorous varieties, such as:

Yellow-flowered: *Nymphaea marliacea chromatella*, 'Moorei', 'Colonel A.J. Welch'.
White-flowered: *Nymphaea alba*, 'Gladstoniana', *Nymphaea marliacea albida*, *Nymphaea odorata alba*.
Pink-flowered: 'Colossea', *Nymphaea marliacea carnea*, 'Masaniello', *tuberosa rosea*.
Red-flowered: 'Attraction', 'Charles de Meurville', 'Conqueror', 'Escarboucle'.

The majority of the water lilies listed above will thrive with up to 120cm (48in) of water above the crown, with the floating leaves spreading

Below: *An informal Koi pond with a strategically positioned Japanese lantern that reflects an Oriental influence in the waterside planting.*

the same distance across the surface of the water. 'Moorei', *marliacea albida, odorata alba*, 'Masaniello', and 'Conqueror' are more suitable for 60-90cm (24-36in) water depth.

If you are starting with the tubers, plant them singly in solid tubs, rather than in the planting baskets normally recommended for goldfish ponds. Fill the container with a heavy loam and add a 2.5cm (1in) layer of coarse gravel on the top to stop the fishes stirring up the soil. Firm the tuber well into the container, with just the growing tip showing above the gravel layer.

Position the pots on bricks or other supports to bring them up to the correct water depth for the variety of water lily concerned.

Oxygenators and floating plants
Oxygenating plants, such as Canadian Pond Weed (*Anacharis canadensis*), Willow Moss (*Fontinalis antipyretica*) and *Lagarosiphon* sp., are widely used in ponds because they literally release oxygen into the water in strong sunlight. The problem in Koi ponds is that the larger Koi will quickly destroy such plants and, for this reason, they are not recommended. Another reason for avoiding a lush growth of oxygenating plants (or any green plants for that matter) in a Koi pond

Above: *A simple Oriental-style bridge straddles the 'arm' of an imaginative Koi pond in concrete.*

is that in the absence of light, i.e. during the night, the plants consume oxygen. This may be particularly crucial during warm summer weather, when the low level of dissolved oxygen in the water coincides with a high oxygen demand by the active fishes.

Floating plants will also be destroyed by Koi, although the so-called Water Soldier, *Stratiotes aloides*, will generally survive in a Koi pond, thriving in alkaline water.

Marginal plants
Many varieties of marginal plants, i.e those that thrive in shallow water, are suitable for Koi ponds so long as they are planted in such a way that the Koi cannot uproot them. Either plant them in large tubs or build brick or stone walls along ledges to retain the soil. Supreme among marginal plants are the many varieties of irises that thrive in wet conditions, notably the Laevigatae.

Below: *A well-stocked European Koi pond landscaped with care to suit both Western and Japanese tastes. The pond is butyl rubber.*

Buying Koi

Always try to buy your fish from a local supplier. That way, you do not have to travel so far if you have subsequent cause for complaint or need further advice. It is also less stressful for the fish if the journey home is a short one. Examine the premises carefully. Do they look clean and well managed? Are the ponds free from dirt and well filtered? Watch how the dealer catches and handles the fish; any rough treatment could lead to trouble with your fish later on.

Points to check
The stock should look active and bright eyed, and should respond immediately to feeding. Fish sulking on the bottom of the pond with closed fins are a sure sign of trouble.

When you have selected your fish, the dealer will put it in a polythene bag. Always insist on giving it a careful examination through the bag before you take it home. Look for parasites, blemishes, missing scales, clamped or diseased fins and sunken eyes. The gills should lie close to the head and should not stand out. The body should be rounded but not bloated. Avoid any fish which has scales standing out from the body: this is a certain indication of dropsy. Never buy an ulcerated fish and do not purchase any other fish from the premises as the rest are probably incubating this bacterial infection.

The best time to buy Koi is in the early autumn, although most fish are sold in the spring. If you are breeding Koi, buy them in the early summer, just as they are coming into season. If you are a beginner, however, it is best not to try breeding Koi; instead buy small fish – 7.5-10cm (3-4in) long – and rear them yourself. Many factors affect the retail price of Koi, but generally, you get what you pay for.

Sources of Koi
Japan Being the home of Koi, Japan produces the best fish. Their colours are brighter, and all the varieties are available in many sizes. Naturally, they are also the most expensive. If you wish to show your Koi, always buy Japanese fish.

Above: *Netting a Koi for closer inspection at a show. The fishes are usually displayed in a blue plastic basket that floats in the water.*

Above: *Small Koi for sale at a show. Fish of this size are ideal for beginners setting up a pond.*

Left: *Koi held in pens at a Koi farm in Japan. The netting is used to provide vital shade to prevent fish literally becoming 'sun burnt'.*

Israel and the USA These fish are cheaper than Japanese Koi. However, they are not line-bred and the colours can be very indistinct.

Singapore This country produces healthy Koi that do not appear to have been affected by the hole-in-the-body disease. The fish are relatively cheap but lack colour.

Europe In Europe there are two types of Koi dealer. The first is a specialist who usually deals with no other fish. If you want top-quality Koi and are prepared to pay the high prices, this is the establishment to visit. The second supplier is a general water gardener who handles all types of coldwater fish and plants, rather than purely Koi. This dealer generally stocks a selection of reasonably priced Koi from various overseas sources.

Quarantine
Never put a newly purchased fish straight into your pond. Although it may seem healthy, the fish might be incubating a disease which could take weeks to appear and could infect the other fish in the pond. If possible, build a quarantine pool; otherwise a large aquarium will do. Keep the new specimen in quarantine for three weeks. In the first week, treat the fish for flukes; in the second week for protozoan parasites, and in the third week for fungus and bacterial infections. (See pages 56-69 for treatments.) If at the end of this period the fish is still fit and healthy, you can introduce it into the main pool.

Transporting fish from abroad
Before the fish is despatched, it is starved to prevent it fouling the water with droppings during

transport. It is then placed in a double-skin polythene bag containing a small amount of water. Oxygen is pumped into the bag, which is then sealed. Large Koi are usually packed individually in an oxygen-filled polythene bag within a stout cardboard box. Keeping the fish cool and dark helps to reduce stress during the journey.

Even so, the fish may be quite stressed when it is first unpacked by the dealer, and it will need a few hours to recover. The next two weeks are critical, as this is the time when a fish may develop all kinds of ailments as a result of the journey. However, with correct medication and feeding, it will soon be restored to top condition. It pays, therefore, to ask your dealer how long the fish has been in the pool. Try to buy fish that have been in stock with the dealer for at least three weeks.

These three photographs show the main stages in buying and taking home a Koi. Left: Having selected your fish, the dealer will net it into a 'baby bath' and then into a plastic bag. Below: Adding oxygen to the bag to sustain the fish on the journey home. Once inflated, the bag is tied at the neck. Right: Float the bag on the surface of your quarantine pool for at least an hour before release.

Transporting fish to your home

Your dealer will place the fish in an air-filled polythene bag, although oxygen may be preferable to air if you have a long journey. A thick polystyrene box, such as is used for importing tropical fish, will keep the fish cool and dark during the trip.

When you arrive home, remove the bag from the box and float the inflated bag in your quarantine pool to allow the water temperature to equalize. Placing a sheet of newspaper over the bag will help reduce shock to the fish when it is exposed to the light. Float the fish for at least an hour, particularly if oxygen has been used. Then open the bag and let the water from the pool slowly mix with the water in the bag. Now release the fish. It will often sulk for a while before beginning to swim normally. If it feeds quickly, this is a good sign.

Feeding

When feeding Koi, the main objectives are to build muscle – keeping the body firm without making the fish fat – and to maintain and enhance the fishes' colour. Koi benefit from being fed as wide a range of foods as possible, but they sometimes take a little time to get used to new foods. In this section, we consider the basic feeding routine, recommended types of foods, and look briefly at the Japanese art of 'iroage'.

Feeding routine

Always feed your Koi in the same place. In this way, they will become very tame and learn to eat from your hand. By bringing the fish in close, you can monitor them for any loss of condition or disease. You will also notice if any of them are missing, which may give you warning that there are hungry herons about.

It is better to underfeed rather than overfeed. Because Koi do not have an organ equivalent to a stomach, they cannot eat a great quantity of food at one time. Therefore, 'little and often' must be the rule. Feeding too much also increases the danger of polluting the pool with uneaten food.

It is normal practice to feed Koi twice a day. For the first meal in the morning, give them an easily digestible food that is high in carbohydrates. The second feed should be in the afternoon or evening and should contain more protein than carbohydrate. In general, Koi kept out of doors do not feed during the winter, although the weather is an important factor.

Processed foods

Koi are omnivorous and eat a wide variety of foods. Most people use

Pelleted foods for Koi

Large floating wheatgerm pellets. The high vegetable content of these pellets makes them easy to digest, even at lower water temperatures.

Large so-called 'staple' pellets. A balanced formulation of fish meal, vegetable protein, minerals and vitamins for everyday feeding.

Medium-sized sinking wheatgerm pellets. Use sinking pellets in cooler conditions, when the fish are less active and at lower levels.

Mini 'staple' pellets. These are ideal for feeding to small fishes. Even smaller 'baby' pellets are available for feeding to very young Koi.

proprietary brands of food, which are generally available as pellets. These are produced in different grades to suit Koi at various sizes, from pellets 1.5mm (0.06in) in diameter for fishes between 5 and 10cm (2-4in) long, to 7mm (0.3in) pellets for fishes over 30cm (12in) long. Standard food contains protein (usually fish-based) plus a mixture of vitamins and minerals. Other processed foods contain vegetable-based protein, such as wheatgerm meal, plus *Spirulina platensis*, a highly nutritious species of filamentous alga from Mexico. *Spirulina* is quickly digested, and thus can be fed at quite low temperatures. It also acts as a 'colour' food, serving to strengthen and 'fix' the coloured areas of the fish. Other pellets may contain carotene, which also acts as an effective colour enhancer.

Pellets may be of the floating or sinking variety. The latter are best for the cooler months, when Koi are not so active.

Live foods
Live foods are greatly in demand by Koi fanciers. Being natural foods, they have a high nutritional value and they also have the advantage that any provided whole and left uneaten will survive and will not pollute the pool. The following live foods are suitable for Koi.

Earthworms Earthworms are the easiest live food to obtain. They can be collected by the dozen at night, especially after rain. All you need is a flashlight and a quick hand. Undisturbed, the worms will remain above ground but quickly retreat into their holes when they sense danger. Another way of collecting

Large 'gold' pellets. The foods on this page are all so-called 'colour-enhancers'. This type contains the orange pigment carotene.

Mini 'gold' pellets, suitable for feeding to smaller fishes. Mini pellets are approximately 2.5mm (0.1in) across. Floating type.

Medium-sized pellets containing a high content of wheatgerm and Spirulina alga. For easy digestion and quick colour enhancement.

Mini 'Spirulina' pellets. These contain a mixture of carotene and Spirulina extract for a quick and effective colour enhancing effect.

worms is to lay a hessian sack in a shady corner of the garden. Place a layer of tea leaves underneath it and keep them wet. The worms will accumulate under the hessian and provide you with a steady supply. It is also possible to breed them in large wooden boxes filled with earth. Feed them with vegetable refuse, such as potato peelings and cabbage leaves. If worm-collecting does not appeal to you, there are companies that specialize in breeding worms for the coarse-fishing market and will sell them in small tubs.

Earthworms are an excellent live food. The small ones can be fed whole, while larger specimens can be cut up before feeding them to the fish. They are easily digestible.

Daphnia These small crustaceans ('water fleas') can be bought from aquatic or pet stores or you can collect them in warm weather from ponds, especially those used by cattle. *Daphnia* swim with a jerky motion and are easy to catch with a fine mesh net. The problem with obtaining *Daphnia* from a wild source is that they may carry parasites and diseases into the pond. While it is possible to breed *Daphnia*, most people find it too troublesome. Obtained from a reliable, disease-free source, *Daphnia* are an excellent food source for fry and young fish, but will be consumed just as readily by adult Koi in the pond.

Tubifex worms These aquatic worms are bright red in colour and up to 5cm (2in) long. They are sold by weight in aquatic stores. In their natural state they live in the mud around sewerage outlets. To avoid introducing disease into the pond, wash worms from a suspect source thoroughly in clean water for several days to evacuate their intestines before feeding them to the fish. To keep *Tubifex* worms alive, place them in a shallow dish under a constantly dripping tap.

Bloodworms These larval stages of midges are blood red in colour and

Above: *Feeding Koi with floating pellets. These fishes are about 10cm (4in) long and are eagerly taking the 'mini' pellets. Use pellets as the basic diet, plus live foods.*

jointed. They swim in a characteristic sideways motion and reach up to 12mm (0.5in) in length. They provide a nutritious live food.

Mosquito larvae These will be found during the warmer months in any stagnant water, such as a rainwater butt. They 'breathe' through the rear part of the body and hang upside-down from the water surface. They are black and usually about 1cm (0.4in) in length, although there are several species and the larvae vary in size. They may be caught with a fine-mesh net and will be greedily accepted by all fish.

Glassworms These transparent larvae – also called Phantom Larvae – float horizontally in the water and move with sharp twisting movements. They may be 1cm (0.4in) long, and again are eagerly sought after by most fishes.

Maggots These are obtainable from fishing tackle shops. Be sure to choose only the white ones and do not buy any that have been dyed.

Water lice These are common in both still and flowing waters and resemble woodlice in appearance. Koi eat them with relish, although only the larger fish seem able to cope with their hard carapace, or outer shell.

Tadpoles If frogs spawn in your pool, the Koi will eat the tadpoles enthusiastically, although they appear to ignore those of the toad.

Plants Duckweed and softer plants such as oxygenating plants will be eaten, but the Koi will not touch marginals and water lilies.

Many of the above animal foods may be bought either in freeze-dried or frozen form. They tend to be rather expensive, but are much safer to use because the irradiation treatment used in their preparation kills off any parasitic or disease-forming organisms.

Iroage
This Japanese term describes the practice of bringing out the best colour potential of your Koi. By caring for the fish in certain ways, and by feeding certain foods, their colour pigments can be enhanced. Iroage foods may contain dried shrimps and algae such as *Chlorella* and *Spirulina*. Always use these foods as directed. If used to excess, *Chlorella* may make the white areas of the fish take on a reddish tinge, for example.

The pond water must be absolutely pure and clean for the Koi to develop their brightest colours. Good filtration, with the addition of activated carbon and zeolite, will help to maintain very clean water. Be sure to remove chlorine with a proprietary chlorine remover whenever the pool is topped up or the water is changed.

Koi show their best colours at lower temperatures, and they will begin to fade in water kept above 27°C (81°F). Since Koi can alter their colour in response to the colour of their surroundings, a black liner is ideal for pool construction.

51

Seasonal care

The amount of time you need to spend on your Koi will vary according to the season of the year. Each month poses different problems, most of which are generally related to the weather.

Spring

This is an exciting time for the Koi enthusiast as it is the beginning of the Koi year. However, your fish will be at their lowest ebb; the fat reserves built up during the previous summer and autumn to tide them over the winter will be all but used up. This, combined with fluctuating temperatures, means that your Koi are most at risk from infection. The water temperature will be about 7°C (45°F) and the fish will not be very active. Ensure that you provide easily digestible food at this time of the year, ideally including carbohydrates and live foods, such as chopped earthworms. If you feed the fish more indigestible foods, and there is a cold spell, they will be carrying half-digested food in their intestines, which could lead to inflammation.

It is a good idea to drain or back-flush your filters before filter activity increases as the bacteria begin to proliferate in the rising temperatures. Expect 'algal blooms' because the plants are not yet growing strongly, filter activity is low, and sunny days will encourage the growth of algae feeding on the nitrates that have accumulated in the pool from winter rains. 'Green water', which consists of millions of microscopic algal cells, should be cleared by the filters. Filamentous algae, or blanket weed, can be more difficult to eradicate. If persistent, it may be killed using a high-grade algicide as directed by the makers. The decaying filaments should then be removed by the filter or you can suck them out with a self-priming vacuum pump (see page 54).

Summer

As far as Koi are concerned, summer begins when the temperature of the water reaches 13°C (55°F). When the temperature reaches 19-24°C (66-75°F), the Koi

Above: *A net screens this pond from the attentions of cats, herons and other potential predators. It also serves to catch autumn leaves.*

will be at their most active. They will look eagerly for food and, if fed correctly, will quickly put on weight. Do not forget that by feeding the fish well now, you will be building up their reserves to face the winter hibernation period. High-protein foods will be appreciated, but remember that the higher levels of nitrogenous wastes produced will

increase the load on the filter
system. Carry out regular water
changes to compensate. The
oxygen content of the water will
decrease, so adjust your aeration
system accordingly.

As the temperature rises,
parasites breed faster and so your
fishes' health should be a major
concern. Observe your fish every
day for signs of infection. It may be
necessary to provide shade on very
hot days if there are no water lilies in
your pool. Strong sunshine will
bleach the colours of your fish.

Early summer is spawning time,
so if you are breeding fish be sure to
get up early to detect signs of
breeding activity (see page 70).

Autumn

At the beginning of autumn, the
water temperature will begin to fall
but your fish will still be feeding well.
At this time, with the sun's rays
weakening, the fishes' colours are at
their best.

In mid-autumn start to make
preparations for the winter. Check
your fish carefully for parasites and

wounds and take appropriate action (see 'Diseases', pages 56-69). With the first frosts, the leaves of aquatic plants will shrivel and die, and these should be removed. Put nets in place to catch falling leaves and to deter herons, which are most active in the misty autumn mornings. (They too want to build up fat reserves).

In late autumn, purify the pool with methylene blue according to the manufacturer's instructions. A good clean up of the bottom of the pool is also advisable. A build up of mulm and leaves will constitute a health hazard to the fish. This should be removed regularly before it decays, either by means of the bottom drain, by netting or, if possible, by siphoning. However, a speedier and more efficient option is to use a self-priming vacuum pump. This is the type used to clean swimming pools and is also ideal for

Koi ponds. The pump is surface mounted and portable, often carried on a small trolley. The flexible suction tube is supported on a long rigid handle and can be used in the same way as a vacuum cleaner, the debris being sucked up to the sump.

Winter

Koi are kept all over the world in a variety of climates. The following safety measures will not apply to those living in warmer countries. Koi are basically very hardy fish that will flourish in temperatures of 2-30°C (36-85°F). Japan has a cold but short winter, which means that extra precautions have to be taken in countries with longer winters, such as Northern Europe and North America. For small fish, this longer period with little or no food puts a greater strain on their fat reserves, and mortality rates will therefore be

Summer

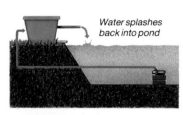

Water splashes back into pond

Winter

Water returned with minimum disturbance

Above: *Since fish survive extreme cold in the wild, it is not surprising to learn that Nature 'provides' during the winter. In the summer, the surface waters are warmest. However, at or below 4°C (about 40°F), the lower levels are slightly warmer than the surface waters, providing a natural refuge for the relatively inactive fishes. The same applies in Koi ponds; avoid disrupting such an ideal system.*

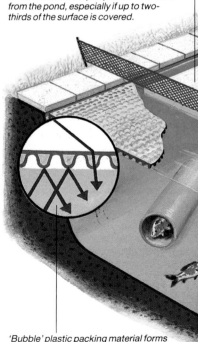

Floating sheets of expanded polystyrene on the water will help to prevent heat loss from the pond, especially if up to two-thirds of the surface is covered.

'Bubble' plastic packing material forms an excellent insulating layer. (The same principle is used for swimming pool covers.) The transparent bubbles allow the sun's rays through but trap the heat.

much higher unless special measures are taken.

When the temperature drops below 7°C (45°F) Koi begin to hibernate. Their metabolism slows down and their heart rate, respiration and digestion become irregular. They do not move around as normal and their appetite declines. Above 13°C (55°F) Koi do not hibernate and will swim and feed normally. Below 2°C (36°F), Koi are at risk and may die.

To prevent the pool freezing over completely, you can install a commercial pool heater to be switched on during cold periods. A pool cover, supported on poles laid across the pool, is useful. Polythene and PVC are both excellent materials for this purpose, but make sure they are secured correctly or the wind will tear them to shreds. In Japan it is common practice to lay flat polystyrene sheets on the pool surface. If you cover two-thirds of the pool, this will prevent a great deal of heat escaping from the water surface. 'Bubble' plastic wrapping material will also act as an efficient insulator. To prevent fishes from becoming stranded on top of these floating sheets, position a net at the margin of the open water, as shown in the illustration below.

If you do feed in winter, use sinking rather than floating food, as Koi seldom rise to the surface in colder weather. And feed only 10-20 percent of the quantity usually given in the summer. It is not advisable to feed Koi when the water temperature is less than 10°C (50°F), however. Leave filters switched on in winter, especially undergravel types. External filters should only be switched off if the conditions are so severe that water freezes as it flows.

Winter care for Koi

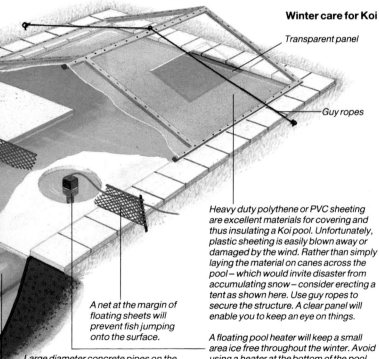

Transparent panel

Guy ropes

Heavy duty polythene or PVC sheeting are excellent materials for covering and thus insulating a Koi pool. Unfortunately, plastic sheeting is easily blown away or damaged by the wind. Rather than simply laying the material on canes across the pool – which would invite disaster from accumulating snow – consider erecting a tent as shown here. Use guy ropes to secure the structure. A clear panel will enable you to keep an eye on things.

A net at the margin of floating sheets will prevent fish jumping onto the surface.

Large diameter concrete pipes on the bottom of the pool are often recommended as winter refuges for Koi. However, the fishes may damage themselves moving in and out of the pipes. Consider the possible hazards.

A floating pool heater will keep a small area ice free throughout the winter. Avoid using a heater at the bottom of the pool because this will cause colder water from the top of the pool to circulate down to the slightly warmer lower levels, thus disrupting the 'layering' of the water that occurs at or below 4°C (about 40°F).

Diseases and predators

The first signs of disease in a fish are usually pretty obvious. A keen fishkeeper can tell a sick fish from a distance, just by its attitude in the water. The fish looks rather miserable and often listless, with folded fins and a lack-lustre look to the body. Other signs include gasping at the surface and quick darting movements, often accompanied by the fish attempting to scrape itself against planting baskets and other hard surfaces.

You are most likely to encounter disease among your stock a short period after purchase. This is because the majority of diseases are triggered by stress. Most Koi are imported and the handling, netting, travelling and overcrowding, together with fluctuating temperatures and water changes, are all obviously upsetting to the fish. This stress often leads to loss of condition and a reduced ability to resist infection. For this reason, it is extremely important to quarantine newly acquired fish (see page 46).

Fish disease is a complex and wide-ranging subject. Here, we consider a selection of the most common diseases and health problems your Koi may encounter. Many other bacterial, parasitic and organic disorders, such as tumours, are common. In many cases, diagnosis without laboratory facilities is impossible.

Before we look at the infections we consider briefly the types of treatment possible.

Methods of treatment
Treatment methods vary according to the disease or problem being tackled, ranging from simply adding

Basic treatment techniques

Above: *These photographs show treatment of an individual fish. These techniques should be undertaken only by a veterinarian or suitably qualified or experienced fishkeepers. Once anaesthetized, (see pages 68-9) this Koi has been laid on a wet towel. Folding the corners of the towel over the head and tail will keep it calm and secure.*

a treatment to the water to delicate surgical techniques that can only be performed by a veterinarian.

Medicated bath Some treatments involve immersing the fish for a short period of, say, 5 minutes, while others take longer. Various chemicals and drugs are added to the water in specific concentrations. Sometimes the fish are removed from the pool for a short bath in the solution. In many cases this is not practical and the whole pond is dosed. This process is repeated until a cure is effected. When adding treatments directly to the pond, it is essential to know the volume of water accurately to calculate the dosage (see the table on page 17).

Oral administration Antibiotics and other specific medicines are often

mixed with food in order to combat various bacterial ailments.

Surface painting This is chiefly used to treat wounds and lesions, but also for body ulcers. In these cases, compounds such as mercurochrome, methylene blue or povidone-iodine are painted on with a fine brush or cotton bud.

Injections These are only used when treating large and valuable fish and should be administered by a veterinarian. Generally, antibiotics are used in the treatment of bacterial infections. Possible injection sites are the muscles behind the pectoral fin and the area behind the vent.

Surgery This is only performed by veterinarians on large and valuable fish, generally to remove tumours.

Above: *Cleaning the site of damage with a cotton bud. This is the first stage of any course of treatment, particularly for wounds and lesions.*

Above: *Applying mercurochrome (or an equivalent preparation such as povidone-iodine) to sterilize. Use mercurochrome with care.*

Above: *Applying a waterproof ointment to the site as the final stage of treatment. Such ointments adhere well to the skin and kill bacteria in the region of the wound.*

Above: *Injecting a Koi, in this case with a general purpose antibiotic. If you are not experienced, ask your veterinarian or local Koi dealer to carry out such specialized tasks.*

Koi diseases and treatment

The following diseases and parasitic infestations that may affect Koi are fairly straightforward to recognize and should respond to the recommended treatment if given correctly and promptly.

Anchor worm (*Lernaea sp.*)

Female anchor worms (the principal parasitic stage of the organism) resemble small twigs, about 20mm (0.8in) long, hanging onto the fishes' body. They occur most often on freshly imported Koi. In the spring, two egg sacs are visible at the end of the long thin body. The organism itself is not a worm but a tiny crustacean, which can be seen more clearly if the 'twig' is carefully pulled out with a pair of tweezers. By piercing the skin, anchor worms expose the fish to secondary infections, which normally create further health problems.

Treatment: Several proprietary treatments are available that can be added to the pond and will kill all the larval stages in the complex life

Below: *An anchor worm is clearly visible on this Koi. As the common name suggests, the adult stage of this crustacean parasite literally 'anchors' itself in the skin.*

cycle of the anchor worm. The most widely available treatments contain the organophosphorus compound dimethyltrichlorohydroxyethyl phosphonate. (This is available under various trade names, including Dipterex, Dylox and Masoten.) Use such treatments strictly according to the directions. (See the table on pages 68-69.)

It is possible to remove the adult parasites by hand using fine tweezers. (This involves anaesthetizing the fish in a suitable bowl or baby bath. See the table for general advice on this procedure. If you are unsure, seek veterinary help.) Treat the wound with mercurochrome or povidone-iodine applied with a soft camel-hair brush or cotton bud. Keep the fish in a fungicidal and bacterial bath until recovery is complete.

Carp pox

This viral disease seems to occur in crowded conditions. It manifests itself as opalescent, greasy-looking white spots that can become quite large. When the infection is at an advanced stage, they merge and take on a reddish grey appearance.

Treatment: If you clean out and thoroughly disinfect the filter, the problem should disappear after

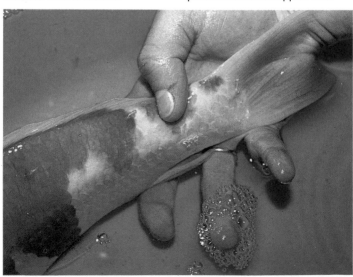

Above: *These greasy blobs are typical of the viral disease carp pox, or skin papilloma. No treatment is available, but affected fishes usually recover in clean conditions.*

eight to twelve weeks. There is no known treatment as such, but the disease is not normally fatal, and will usually cure itself in time.

Cloudy eye

With this disease, one or both eyes may become clouded over and opaque. A fish will lose its appetite and become listless. This is a non-specific infection and may be caused by parasitic as well as bacterial infections.

Treatment: Make sure that the conditions are as clean and healthy as possible and add a little salt to the water – at the rate of 3gm per litre (0.5oz per gallon). If a parasite, such as *Oodinium* (velvet disease), is detected then treat it with an appropriate antiparasitic remedy. Otherwise use an antibacterial.

Columnaris

(*Flexibacter columnaris*)
This is a virulent bacterial disease, misleadingly referred to as 'mouth fungus' because of the greyish white film it produces. It usually attacks the head region, which can result in the mouthparts and adjacent areas being eaten away, but it can attack any part of the body. It is highly contagious.

Treatment: Remove all affected fish from the pool at once. Place them in a weak salt solution and keep the water very clean by filtration. Sterilize all nets and utensils after use. Products containing phenoxyethanol, nifurpirinol, nitrofurazone and benzalkonium chloride are some recommended treatments. Follow the guidelines on pages 68-69.

Below: *This greyish white film is caused by the bacterial infection* Columnaris. *Typically found on the head region, it may also affect other parts of the fish, as shown here.*

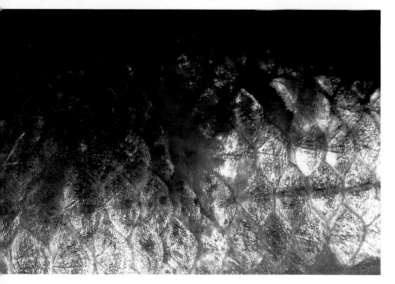

Dropsy (*Ascites*)

Dropsy is often known as 'pine-cone disease' because one of the symptoms is that the scales stand out from the body. The chief characteristic, however, is a swollen abdomen. Affected fishes also swim and breathe with difficulty. Eventually the eyes and head also become swollen. Various bacteria are responsible for this condition, which is normally fatal. However, a

Above: *The swollen abdomen and protruding scales are clear signs of dropsy, a bacterial infection that may prove fatal if not treated.*

cure may be attempted and this is sometimes effective.

Treatment: Antibacterial treatment and salt baths are worth trying. Using oxolinic acid to make medicated food may also help.

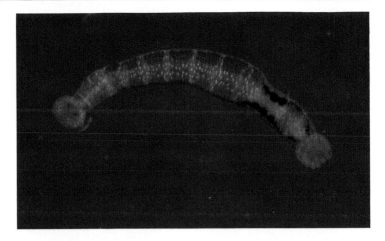

Finrot and tailrot (*Aeromonas hydrophila* and other species) This condition generally occurs when the fish are living in unsatisfactory conditions. The bacteria are normally present on the fish, and only attack as a result of damage or stress caused during travelling and handling. The first symptom is the appearance of opaque patches on the fins, but the infection quickly develops to an acute stage when the fins rot away, leaving bloody fin rays. Ultimately, the entire fin is destroyed and the body itself is attacked. At this stage, the fish is doomed to die. As with other diseases, the affected fish is vulnerable to attack by secondary fungal, viral or bacterial infections.

Treatment: Consult your veterinarian, who may anaesthetize the fish and cut away the infected portions of the fins. Providing the disease is caught early enough, phenoxyethanol, nifurpirinol, nitrofurazone, benzalkonium chloride and chloramine are effective. Follow the manufacturer's instructions when using these.

Left: *Koi with signs of finrot. Unchecked, the infection (caused by various bacteria) eventually causes the fins to disintegrate and may then spread onto the body. Use proprietary remedies as directed and maintain clean conditions in the pond.*

Above: *A fish leech,* Piscicola geometra, *in a 'relaxed' position. When 'extended', it may reach up to 3cm (1.2in) in length. Leeches in general do not usually pose a serious health problem in Koi ponds, although they can pass on infections and cause body damage that may become infected.*

Fish leech (*Piscicola geometra*) There are dozens of species of freshwater leeches, but they seldom cause any problem to the fish. However, occasionally a pond may become infested with the dangerous types. Fish leeches are worm-like, but flattened, and they crawl and swim in a series of looping motions. Infected fish will rub themselves vigorously against hard objects. Close inspection may reveal the presence of leeches, which may be up to 3cm (1.2in) long, clinging to the body. They are normally brown or greyish in colour.

Treatment: Remove the fish from the pool and place it in a three percent salt solution for a short time. The leeches will either drop off or may be removed gently by hand. (After about ten minutes the fish will become unconscious and should be removed at once.) Do not attempt to remove the leeches without first using the salt, or the mouth parts may be left in the skin, giving rise to nasty infections. Clearing the pool is more difficult.

61

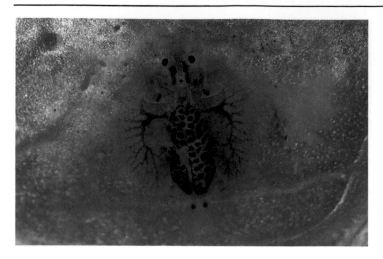

Fish lice (*Argulus* sp.)

The fish louse is a common parasite on newly imported Koi. It is a parasitic crustacean 8-12mm (0.3-0.5in) in diameter, and is easily recognizable with the naked eye. It attaches itself to the fish by its paired suckers and draws blood from the fish through a needle-like proboscis, causing inflammation and anaemia.

Treatment: Treat the pond water with a course of a proprietary preparation containing dimethyltricholorohydroxyethyl phosphonate, such as Dipterex, Dylox or Masoten. Treating individual fish involves using a short-term bath (see table) and dabbing mercurochrome or povidone-iodine on the wounds.

Above: *A fish louse,* Argulus foliaceus, *clinging to the skin. The suckers, the parasite's means of attachment, look like eyes.*

Fungus (Principally *Saprolegnia*)
This disease first appears in small patches resembling cotton wool. They often occur on the site of an injury. Although normally white, the presence of unicellular algae will often give the fungal growth a greenish appearance. Once it takes a hold, it can quickly cover the entire body. The fungal filaments are anchored in the skin and absorb nutrients from the fishes' body.

Below: *A Koi with fungal growths attached to the skin. Their green appearance is caused by the accumulation of green algal cells.*

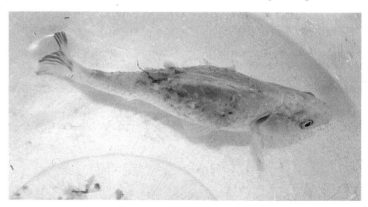

Treatment: Use a mixture of malachite green and common salt, or malachite green and formalin as shown in the table on pages 68-69.

Gill flukes
(*Dactylogyrus* and other species)
Koi heavily infested with gill flukes show an increased respiratory rate and gaping gills. The fish will 'mouth' at the surface. The organisms responsible are very small worm-like creatures known as monogenetic trematodes. (The term 'monogenetic' means that their parasitic life cycle occurs entirely in one host.) The parasites, each up to 1mm (0.04in) long, attach to the gills by hooks and can soon devastate the gill filaments if left untreated.

Treatment: Use one of the many good proprietary antiparasitic treatments available as directed.

Pop-eye (*Exophthalmus*)
With this disease, one or both eyes begin to protrude progressively from the socket. In the later stages of the disease, the eye may be expelled and blindness occurs. This condition can be caused by many organisms.

Treatment: A combination of antiparasitic and antibacterial treatments may be effective.

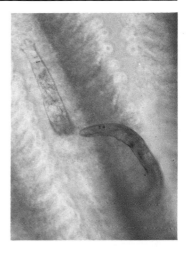

Above: *A microphotograph showing two gill flukes* (Dactylogyrus *sp.)* *attached to the gill filaments. A heavy infestation causes gaping gills and may lead to permanent damage if left untreated. Gill flukes are a particular hazard for baby fishes and for adults in a weakened condition. Treatment is effective.*

Below: *Protruding eyes, a condition known as 'pop-eye', may result from a variety of causes. These include certain parasites invading the eye (larval trematodes responsible for worm cataracts), bacterial infections and dropsy.*

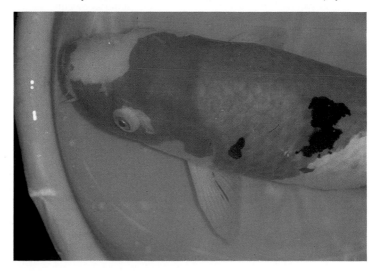

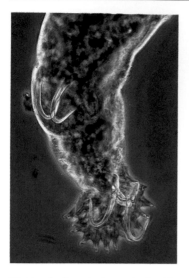

Above: *A microphotograph of a skin fluke,* Gyrodactylus sp. *The hooks are clearly visible at the base, as are those of a juvenile inside the adult.*

Skin flukes (*Gyrodactylus*)
These trematode parasitic worms are closely related to gill flukes (*Dactylogyrus* sp.). Affected fish will rub themselves against hard objects, often with a skimming motion, in their efforts to relieve the irritation caused by the flukes embedded in the skin. Each fluke may be up to 0.8mm (0.03in) long. The skin of affected fishes loses its sparkle and appears whitish or inflamed.

Treatment: Use a proprietary antiparasitic remedy as instructed by the manufacturer.

Sliminess of the skin (Unicellular parasites such as *Costia, Chilodonella, Trichodina* sp.) These parasites cause the skin to take on a greyish appearance as the fish produces excess mucus in reaction to their presence. Affected fishes will rub against hard objects or against the bottom of the pond in their irritation.

Treatment: Broad-spectrum antiparasitic chemicals are effective against these unicellular parasites.

To treat the pond water use a mixture of malachite green and formalin following the guidelines in the table on pages 68-69.

Swimbladder trouble
This is one of the most common problems with the Carp family. Affected fish are unable to maintain their balance and may assume unnatural positions in the water. They may swim head down, upside down, or may even be unable to move off the bottom of the pool. Sometimes the problem has its origins in bacterial infection, but in carp it may be due to an organic malfunction of the swimbladder.

Treatment: There is no definite cure for this condition. However, placing the fish in shallower, warmer water to which a small dose of salt is added, can sometimes result in a cure, although the fish may suffer permanent after-effects.

Tapeworms
These internal parasites often have complex life cycles. *Bothriocephalus acheilognathi* is a species that has been found in some batches of imported fish. Common in China and Japan, it has now spread to many sites in Europe. The adult stage in Koi can cause blockage, intestinal perforation and peritonitis. Some tapeworms, such as *Ligula intestinalis*, infest Koi only as an intermediate host in the cycle.

Treatment: Consult a veterinarian who may use praziquantel or a similar drug to treat infested fish.

Ulcer disease
Infection is due to several species of bacteria, including the *Aeromonas* and *Pseudomonas* species. It has led to great losses in the commercial world during the last ten years. Shallow open sores appear on the body, the base of the fins and sometimes the anus. Although the lesions are superficial, they increase rapidly, leading to chronic septicaemia (blood poisoning), dropsy and death. A great deal of research has been carried out on

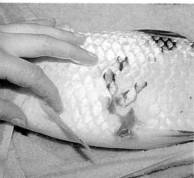

Above: *Cleaning out a 'natural-type' pond revealed these emaciated fishes, two Goldfishes and one Koi, with worms. Such parasites rarely occur in well-kept ponds.*

Left: *Evidence of 'hole disease', which has similar symptoms to ulcer disease. Both of these bacterial infections cause lesions in the body which, if left untreated, can lead to the death of the fish.*

Below: *A severe ulcer has formed on the lower body surface of this Koi.*

this disease but with little success. It is highly contagious, and sick fish should be isolated at once. Fish can be carriers without showing overt symptoms of the disease.

Treatment: Antibiotics or oxolinic acid added to the food seem to be the most effective cure. Salt is useful as a supportive treatment.

White spot disease, or ich
(*Ichthyophthirius*)
This well-known condition (known in Japan as 'Hakuten'), is caused by a unicellular parasite that infests fish at the free-swimming stage of its life cycle. The parasites burrow into the skin and live just beneath the outer skin layer, causing the body and fins to become covered in small white spots about 1mm (0.04in) in diameter. If left untreated, secondary infections, both bacterial and fungal, become established and eventually kill the fish. Untreated fish can die in just a few days or may linger on for weeks.

Treatment: Use a white spot proprietary remedy, malachite green, or malachite green and formalin as indicated on pages 68-69. The treatment works more quickly if the water temperature is raised to at least 26°C (79°F). Increase the aeration to compensate for the lower oxygen levels in warmer water.

Koi predators
If you live in a rural area, predators can be a great problem. Herons, in particular, can wipe out a pool in a couple of mornings. These birds often fly a considerable distance from their natural habitat to suburban back gardens, where they will cause havoc in unprotected pools. Herons attack at sunrise and they generally choose mornings when there is no wind. They also prefer misty or foggy conditions. The only solution is to net the pool.

Below: *A close-up view of the distinctive symptoms of white spot disease, or ich, on a fin. The spots are single-celled parasites growing just beneath the outer layer of the skin. The characteristically curved nucleus can be seen clearly in some of the cells shown here.*

Kingfishers pose a similar problem, although they are seldom found more than a few hundred metres from the stream or pool where they live. Unlike herons, they can only take small fish. Again, netting is the only answer.

Cats are often blamed for catching ornamental fish, but in fact only a few are prepared to get their paws wet. However, those that do learn the trick can be very destructive. 'Cat pepper' or a lively dog will normally deter even the most determined feline fisher.

Koi fry are also attacked by many insect larvae, such as those of the Dragonfly and the Great Diving

Beetle. Both of these larvae reach a length of about 5cm (2in) and will attack and damage fish up to their own length. The adult Great Diving Beetle (*Dytiscus marginalis*) is also a threat to the young fish. Hydra – a graceful yet voracious relative of jellyfishes sporting tentacles bristling with tiny paralyzing stinging cells – can cause heavy losses among newly hatched fry. Other enemies around the world include weasels, snakes, fishing eagles, seagulls and terrapins.

Right: *The adult Great Diving Beetle* (Dytiscus marginalis), *looking like an underwater monster. Such beetles can be a threat to very small fry.*

Below: *The larval stage of the same beetle can easily tackle fish fry up to its own length of 5cm (2in).*

Guidelines for using chemicals

Chemical	Concentration mg/litre (ppm)	Dosage range per 100 litres
Benzalkonium chloride	Bath: 1-4	0.2-0.8ml
Chloramine T	Bath: 2.2 Pool: 0.5	0.2gm 0.05gm
Dimethyltrichloro-hydroxyethyl-phosphonate	Bath: 22 Pool: 0.3	2.2gm 0.03gm
Formalin (A solution containing approx. 37% formaldehyde)	Bath: 24 Pool: 13.5	2.4ml 1.3ml
Formalin and malachite green mixture	Pool: Formalin 15 and malachite green 0.05	1.5ml of mixture
Levamisole	Bath: 10	1gm
Malachite green	Bath: 0.4 (*1) Pool: 0.2 (*1)	2ml 1ml
Methylene blue	Bath: 2(*2)	8ml
MS 222 Anaesthetic	Bath: 25-100	2.5-10gm
Ni furpirinol	Bath: 1-4 Pool: 0.25	0.1-0.4gm 0.025gm
Nitrofurazone	Bath: 1-3	0.1-0.3gm
Oxolinic acid	5gm per kg of treated food	Give treated food at rate of 1% of fish body weight per day
Oxytetracycline	Bath: 13-120 In food: 50mg per kg of fish	1.3-12gm
Para-chloro-phenoxyethanol	Bath: 20	1.8ml
Phenoxyethanol	Bath: 100 Food: Soak in 1% solution (10gm/litre)	9.1ml
Sodium chloride (Common salt)	Bath: 30,000 (3%)	3kg
	Bath/Pool: 10,000(1%)	1kg
	Pool: 3,000(0.3%)	300gm

(*1) Parts per million (ppm) based on solid. Dosages based on 2% solution in water.
(*2) ppm based on solid. Dosages based on 2.5% solution in water. To convert dosages for 100 Imperial gallons and 100 US gallons, multiply figures in 'Dosage range' column by

Treatment time	Other details	Effective against
60 mins	Dosage based on liquid formulation containing 50% active ingredient	Columnaris, finrot, tail-rot and other external bacterial diseases
60 mins Continuous until cured. Repeat after 3 days	Available as powder. Maximum of 3 consecutive treatments	Slime disease, white spot, skin flukes, myxobacterial gill disease, external bacterial diseases
60 mins Continuous until cured. In hard water repeat after 7 days	Maximum 3 consecutive treatments. Products: Dipterex, Dylox, Masoten, Neguvon, Trichlorphon	Fish lice, anchor worms and other parasites, such as skin and gill flukes
30 mins Continuous until cured. Repeat after 7 days	Rarely used alone. Normally used with malachite green, see below. Aerate water	Combined with malachite green: fungus, slime disease, white spot, skin and gill flukes
Continuous until cured	Use 3.3gm of malachite green solid in one litre of formalin	Fungus, slime disease, white spot, and skin and gill flukes
12-24 hours		Intestinal worms
30 mins Continuous until cured. Repeat after 7 days	Use with formalin or sodium chloride	Fungus, slime disease, white spot, other parasites, such as skin flukes
Continuous until cured	Do not use with biological filters; it will disrupt their action	Traditional treatment for fungus, protozoan parasites. Commercial remedies better
1-3 mins, depending on pH, temperature, size and condition of fish	Requires care. Consult veterinarian or other skilled person	
60 mins Continuous until cured	If difficult to obtain, consider using para-chloro-phenoxyethanol	Columnaris, finrot, tailrot, plus other bacterial and fungal diseases
60 mins	If difficult to obtain, consider using para-chloro-phenoxyethanol	Columnaris, finrot, tailrot, plus other bacterial and fungal diseases
Use for 10 days	Available ready mixed with food; take advice from veterinarian	Dropsy, ulcer disease, plus other bacterial diseases
Continuous until cured Use for 7 days	Antibiotic. Use lower concentration unless hard water reduces effect	Bacterial diseases
Continuous until cured	Take care to dissolve and disperse throughly	Fungus, finrot, tailrot, and other bacterial diseases
Continuous until cured Use for 7 days	Supplied as oily liquid Take care to dissolve and disperse thoroughly	Fungus, columnaris, finrot, tailrot. Use soaked food against nematode worms
Up to 10 mins	Remove fish immediately if it shows distress	Cloudy eye and parasites. (Increases mucus flow)
1-2 weeks	Use with malachite green or phenoxyethanol	Supportive for various diseases and wounds/ulcers
Continuous until cured		General protection, e.g. against nitrite toxicity*

4.55 and 3.79 respectively. Internationally accepted chemical names used where possible. Local regulations affect availability of drugs. Seek veterinary advice.

Breeding and showing

Breeding Koi starts with the selection of the parent stock. Males should be at least two years old and females should be over three years of age. The stock does not need to be of show quality in order to produce a proportion of well-coloured youngsters. In fact, show quality Koi and prize winners are seldom used for breeding since it is a very hectic business which may lead to loss of scales and a deterioration in condition.

Spawning and rearing

Male Koi are slender, with a comparatively large head and pectoral fins. When in breeding condition, tubercles (white dots) appear on the pectoral fins and on the gill plates. Female Koi are fatter and can appear slightly lop-sided since the spawn often hangs more heavily on one side of the body than the other. It is usual to mate one female to two or three males, as this ensures a higher fertilization rate.

Koi lay between 100,000 and 750,000 eggs, depending on the size and condition of the female. The eggs are a transparent greenish

Below: *Koi spawning among ropes and conifer branches. The sticky greenish eggs readily adhere to the strands of the spawning medium.*

colour and only about 0.33mm (approximately 0.01in) in diameter. They are sticky and adhere to any finely divided material. Spawning mats may be synthetic, such as nylon brushes, or they can be natural materials, such as water plants and conifer branches. Many breeders use the Water Hyacinth (*Eichhornia crassipes*), which has highly suitable long trailing roots.

While fish can spawn in the pool in which they live, it is more usual to prepare a special breeding pool. Ideally this pool should be about 2.4x1.8m (8x6ft) and 45cm (18in) deep, with the spawning medium placed at one end. When you see that your breeders are ready to spawn, net them carefully and place them in the breeding pool. Do not feed them during this period. Courtship normally occurs during

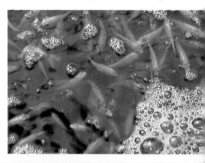

the morning hours, with the female being continually chased by the males as they drive her towards the spawning ground. As soon as spawning has finished, remove the breeders quickly as they will attempt to eat the eggs.

Remove the eggs (still attached to the spawning medium) and place them in a solution of malachite green of a concentration 1:300,000. Leave them for fifteen minutes to disinfect them and then put them back in the breeding pond to hatch. At 21-24°C (70-75°F), they will hatch in four to seven days. Lower or higher temperatures will slow down or speed up the hatching rate respectively. Two or three days after hatching, the fry will become free swimming.

Newly hatched brineshrimp or sifted *Daphnia* are the best first

Left: *A mass of Koi fry in a breeding pond. Overcrowding can lead to cannibalism and spread of disease.*

Below: *Selected young Koi being groomed for possible international stardom on a Japanese Koi farm.*

foods. Keep them on these foods for about a month before weaning them on to suitable dried foods.

Culling
Young Koi should be separated by colour at the age of one month. This is the start of the process of selecting the best individuals for subsequent rearing. Do not attempt to rear all the Koi: select only those that you can comfortably house and discard the unwanted individuals. (The most humane way of killing fish is to chill them with ice cubes.) Keep only 10-20 percent of the fish. Overcrowded fry become cannibalistic and are prone to disease, which can spread quickly.

Showa may be selectively culled after only 14 days. Wait 50 days for Ogon, and 60 days for Kohaku and Taisho Sanke. Weed out all plain white fish and any with deformities. Do not forget that culling is carried out for pattern and quality, and only experience can guide you in this extremely important selection process.

As the fish grow up, further culling is necessary until, by the time they

reach 7.5cm (3in) in length, hopefully you will have selected some interesting possibilities in terms of colour and pattern.

Koi societies and showing
In Japan there are both professional and amateur societies where people with a common interest in Koi culture can meet to discuss ideas, new varieties, breeding techniques and so on. Huge shows are held, which attract thousands of

devotees. The prizes are enormous, and the value of prizewinning fish can increase dramatically.

Since the fervour for Koi-keeping has spread around the world, equivalent shows are proving extremely popular in many countries outside Japan.

Show committees issue a show schedule which lists the classes of Koi to be judged. Rules vary as to the sizes of the fish permitted to enter according to the Koi-keeper's

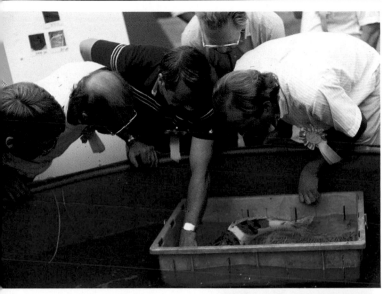

These three photographs reflect the process of judging and the array of prizes on offer at a typical European Koi Show. Open to the public as well as to the owners of the competing Koi, these shows are a market place for fish and equipment as well as a competitive arena, and attract literally thousands of people. Left: Judges consider the Koi displayed in one of the round vats. Above: The judges home in on a potential winner isolated in a floating basket. Right: Accolades in abundance await the winners during the day.

society in question. In Japan, categories may start at up to 18cm (7in) and progress through 10cm (4in) steps to a class for fish over 75cm (30in) in length. Outside Japan, where the Koi are more modestly sized, the size categories typically start with a class for Koi up to 15cm (6in) in length and progress by 10cm steps to a final category for fish over 55cm (22in) in length.

Koi for judging are displayed in round blue vats, about 2-3m (6-10ft) in diameter and with water about 50cm (20in) deep. Several fish are placed in each container and are judged against one another. The judges use their wide experience to decide on the winners and the

runners-up. However, there are moves afoot to introduce a points system similar to that used in the judging of other types of fish.

If you are seriously interested in keeping Koi, be sure to join a society. You will gain many helpful tips on how to condition your fish for a show, how to net them without causing damage, how to pack and transport them and, of course, simply how to maintain and enjoy these most fascinating fishes.

Varieties of Koi

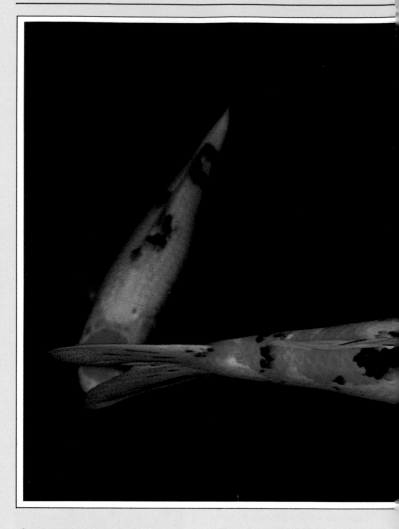

If you are just starting to embrace the culture of Nishikigoi, either as a full-blown hobby or simply as an added attraction to your water garden, you may be bewildered by the mysterious Japanese names given to the individual varieties. Unfortunately 'Westernised' names have not been adopted by the Koi fraternity, so we must identify the different types by their Oriental names. Of course, all these names can be translated, but the translation is normally more long-winded and difficult to remember than the correct Japanese name. This section adopts a simplified approach to presenting Koi types, i.e. by the number of colours they possess. However, to help you progress further in your knowledge of Koi, we have also included the Japanese classification system, which is based on breeding relationships.

Of course, reading a book is one thing, but it is no substitute for observing the fish at first hand. This more than anything will help you

sort the different varieties into 'boxes in your mind'. It is essential, therefore, to visit as many Koi establishments as you possibly can and to ask about any Koi that you cannot identify. Most dealers will be only too happy to help you expand your knowledge of these wonderful creatures.

Initially, you may be drawn to the one-colour metallic fish, such as the gold, silver, platinum or orange 'Ogons'. You may also appreciate the blue and red 'Asagi' and 'Shusui' types. Later, you will learn to appreciate the subtleties of the colour distribution on 'Kohaku' and other more complex varieties.

Finally, do not be ashamed of your lack of knowledge. Even experienced dealers and keen hobbyists had to start from scratch like you, so do not be afraid to ask for that 'gold one' or the one with 'red and white on it'. The dealer will understand and will name the fish correctly when packing it for you.

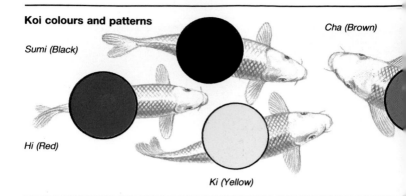

Koi colours and patterns

Sumi (Black)

Cha (Brown)

Hi (Red)

Ki (Yellow)

As mentioned in the first chapter, all Koi are developed from but a single species: the Common Carp (*Cyprinus carpio*). However, various mutations, such as the Mirror Carp of Europe, were crossbred with the original and it is from the type species, plus mutations, that all the current varieties are derived. These varieties have been given Japanese names which might prove confusing at first. However, these names are built up logically from 'components' that may refer to the period in which the variety was developed or to the colour, scale lustre, scale orientation, and finally to the pattern and distribution of colours.

Unlike other animals that breeders have developed along pedigree lines, Koi do not breed true. Having a pair of expensive show winners still means that from 40,000 fry from an adult pair, only about 20 might prove to be fish with acceptable standards of colour and pattern. Remember, too, that not all fish can be given a definite name and that many low grade fish will not fit into the recognized categories.

While the Goldfish has been deliberately bred for bizarre forms of fins, body and eyes, Koi breeders have concentrated on differences in the formation of scales, colour and patterning. However, this may change as Koi become 'international'; already, comet-tailed Koi are being produced. For simplicity, the Koi featured in this section of the book are presented according to the number of colours they have in their make-up. This

cuts across the traditional Japanese system of grouping Koi based on their genealogy, but it does form a useful way of introducing the range of Koi in a fairly straightforward manner. For reference, the Japanese groups are listed at the end of the section, on page 113.

First, we consider the scale types and then the colours in detail, with a selection shown in photographs.

Scale types
Four types of scale formation are recognized among the Koi varieties:

1 Scaled The most common fish with typical carp scales.

2 Doitsu A fish with scales along the dorsal and lateral lines only.

3 Leather A fish with no visible scales, except possibly very small scales along the dorsal line only.

4 Gin Rin A normally scaled fish which has a gold or silvery mirror like effect on the individual scales.

Colour types
This section is divided quite simply into single-colour, two-colour and three-colour fishes, with a mention of a multicolour type. The selection features the most important varieties available, plus a few of the more 'specialized' and rare ones. New ones are being developed all the time. Just to confuse matters, a single variety may be known by more than one name according to various authorities.

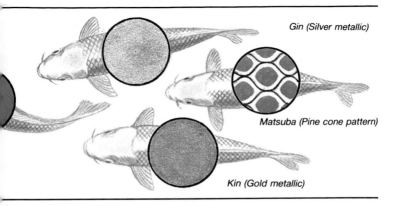

Gin (Silver metallic)

Matsuba (Pine cone pattern)

Kin (Gold metallic)

DESCRIPTIVE TERMS USED FOR KOI

The simplest terms used to name different varieties of Koi are the colours. Even here, though, confusion can arise. There are three terms for red, for example: 'Aka', 'Beni' and 'Hi'. The first two refer to an overall red colour, in conjunction with other descriptive terms, while the third is used to describe patches of red (on a white fish, for example). A similar situation arises with black, where 'Karasu' is used for a totally black fish and 'Sumi' for black patches. The list of common terms shown on this page will help you to understand how Koi names are built up, sometimes from a combination of several descriptive terms.

Aka	Red	**Muji**	Self-coloured
Akame	Eye with red iris		(literally 'nothing
Beni	Orange-red		else')
Bekko	Tortoiseshell	**Nezu**	Grey
Cha	Brown	**Ogon**	One-colour metallic
Doitsu	German type fish	**Orenji**	Orange
	with scales along	**Parrachina**	Very white metallic
	dorsal and lateral		(Platinum)
	lines only	**Rin**	Scale
Gin	Silver metallic	**Sanke, or**	Three-coloured fish,
Goi	Koi (short form of	**Sanshoku**	normally red, black
	Goior Koi)		and white
Hi	Red	**Shiro**	White
Inazuma	Lightning pattern	**Showa**	Era from 1926
Kabuto	Cap or helmet,		onwards
	referring to fish with	**Shusui**	Old variety from
	a head colour		1868-1926
	different from the	**Sui**	Water (rippling
	body		effect)
Karasu	Black (overall)	**Sumi**	Black (in the form of
Ki	Yellow		a patch)
Kin	Gold metallic	**Taisho**	Era 1912-1926
Kohaku	Red and white fish	**Tancho**	A bird (Tancho zura)
Kuchibeni	Red-lipped		with a red crest
Kujaku	Multicoloured	**Utsuri**	Reflecting
	(Peacock)	**Yamabuki**	Japonica bush with
Matsuba	Pine cone pattern		pale yellow flowers

77

Single-colour Koi

Above: *A mixed group of single-colour Koi, always popular* *throughout the world. The main photograph shows a superb gold*

Ogon (bottom left), a Parrachina (bottom right), a Kigoi (top left) and a Chagoi (top right). The inset features a Parrachina and a Benigoi.

Single-colour Koi may be some of the earliest varieties bred by direct mutation from the common carp or may be throwbacks as a result of crossbreeding multicoloured fish. They can be stunning in appearance.

WHITE

Shiromuji: Produced as a result of breeding Kohaku (Red on White), these fish are normally culled out or discarded when young due to their uninspiring appearance.

RED

Benigoi: Derived from the Kohaku, this fish shows only red coloration.

Below: **Kigoi**
A very attractive yellow Koi.

Hi Matsuba: Basically plain red but with the Matsuba pattern of darker scales giving a pine-cone effect.

YELLOW

Kigoi: These are produced from Asagi (Blue) or Kohaku (Red on White). The colour is a deep yellow in the best specimens, but is contaminated with white in poorer ones. Other varieties are Ki Matsuba, which is a prized fish with the Matsuba pine-cone effect picked out in blue on a yellow base-colour. Akame Kigoi is a yellow Koi with red eyes. Chagoi is a rare variety possessing a buff coloration. The Doitsu form sports a handsome pattern of large scales.

Below: **Chagoi**
A subtle shade of brownish-buff.

Right: **Ginrin Benigoi**
A rich red coloration combined with the 'mother of pearl' scales sparkling along the dorsal surface.

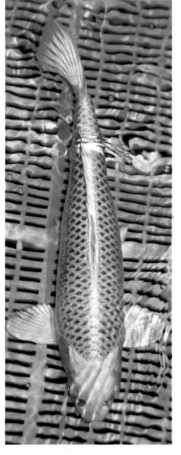

Above: **Kin Matsuba**
*The Matsuba pattern in brown
overlaid on a colour of sheer gold.*

Above: **Ogon**
*A stunning gold fish that is always
one of the most popular varieties.*

METALLIC

Ogon: Ogons are metallic Koi which are normally scaled, but which can be Doitsu or leather.

Kin Matsuba/Matsuba Ogon: This variety has a ground colour of gold with the Matsuba pattern of brown scales with gold edges along the back of the fish. This Matsuba type is derived from Asagi (Blue Koi).

Left: **Parrachina (Leather)**
A widely acclaimed variety with a smooth platinum-white sheen.

Parrachina/Shiro Ogon: This platinum variety is a result of a cross between Nezu-Ogon and an Akami Kigoi. It is probably one of the most popular varieties. (The word 'Parrachina' means 'very white metallic', i.e. suggesting a brilliant platinum effect.)

Gin Matsuba: This attractive platinum fish has the Matsuba (pine cone) pattern picked out in blue.

Orenji Ogon: An attractive fish that combines the metallic lustre of the Ogon with a basic orange colour. This form was first bred in 1956.

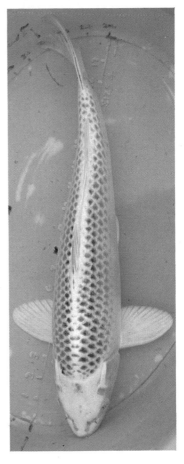

Above: **Orenji Ogon**
An impressive variety of a rich orange with a patina of gold.

Above: **Gin Matsuba**
A subtle mix of platinum overlaid with the Matsuba pattern.

Two-colour Koi

Above: *A group shot featuring the following two-colour varieties of*

Koi: Inazuma Kohaku (large red and white fish); Shiro Bekko (mainly

white with black markings); Shiro
Utsuri (black with white markings);

Hi Utsuri (red and black); and Asagi
(light blue reticulated and red).

Two-colour Koi are designated by such terms as 'Black on Red' or 'Red on Black', which reflect the different parentages involved.

RED ON WHITE

Kohaku: Kohaku is the main pedigree line. It is a white Koi with red patterns. In most Koi contests in Japan the grand champion is a Kohaku. It was first named in 1899. The finest examples of Kohaku have a deep red coloration (Hi) in a sharp and distinct pattern. The white skin should be pure, with no stains or other blemishes. Unless the white is as pure as snow, the red pattern, no matter how good, will be reduced in value considerably. Sometimes black specks, known as 'Shimi', appear in the skin. The overall pattern should be balanced, with an interesting Hi marking that starts at the head and finishes near the tail.

The distance of white skin between the last Hi pattern and the tail is called 'Bongiri', which means 'tail closeout'.

There are many recognized types of Kohaku, including the folllowing:

Kuchibeni Kohaku: Kohaku with a red lipstick-like coloration of the lips. Not easily noticed from above.

Tancho Kohaku: Here, the body is basically white with a large circular red pattern, representing the sun, on the head. A very striking 'design'.

Nidan Kohaku: This name is given to Kohaku having a two-step pattern of red, i.e. two separate areas of colour on the white background.

Right: **Nidan Kohaku**
Two clear patches of red on white.

Below: **Tancho Kohaku**
A simple but very elegant pattern.

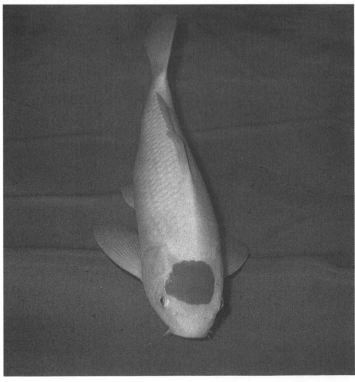

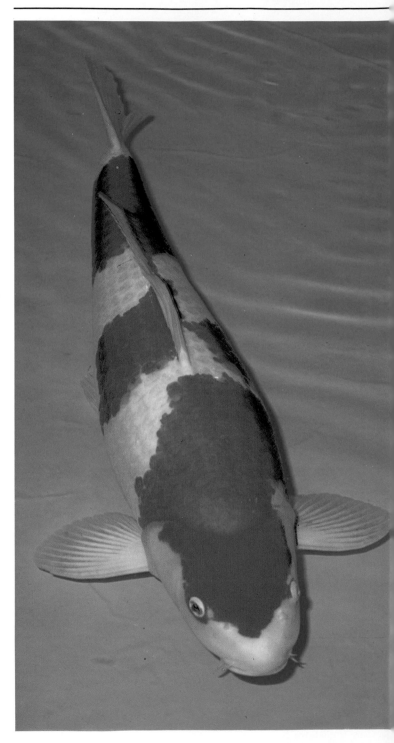

Left: **Sandan Kohaku**
A fine 'three-step' form of Kohaku.

Sandan Kohaku: Kohaku with a three-step pattern of red.

Below: **Yondan Kohaku**
Four red patterns on a white ground.

Yondan Kohaku: These fish have a four-step pattern of red.

Inazuma Kohaku: The word 'Inazuma' means lightning and is applied to Kohaku with a zig-zag pattern of red extending from head to tail. When the Inazuma patterns are large, the fish is called Omoyo; when small, the name Komoyo applies. An impressive variety.

Maruten Kohaku: Kohaku with an isolated Hi marking on the head (similar to that on the Tancho Kohaku – see photo on page 86) plus a Hi marking on the body.

Makibara Kohaku: In this type the red pattern extends around the stomach area.

Kanoko Kohaku: When the red pattern is dappled over the white body, not in a symmetrical way.

Goten-zakura Kohaku: When the spotted red pattern resembles clusters of grapes.

Kinzakura Kohaku: When the Gotenzakura scales are fringed with golden glints.

BLACK ON WHITE

Shiro Bekko: This type of Koi has a white body colour overlaid with blue-black markings (Sumi) that are mottled and extend into the fins but not into the head. Individuals with clear white fins and jet-black sumi markings are considered superior.

BLACK ON RED

Aka Bekko: This variety ideally has a deep red body with black mottling, which can extend into the fins.

Right: **Inazuma Kohaku**
A classic 'lightning' pattern of red.

Above: **Shiro Bekko**
White with black (Sumi) patches.

Left: **Maruten Kohaku**
One of several Kohaku varieties.

BLACK ON YELLOW

Ki Bekko: This is a striking yellow fish with black markings.

WHITE ON BLACK

Shiro Utsuri: This fish has white markings on a Sumi (black) background, giving a more marbled effect than in the Shiro Bekko. It was produced in 1925.

RED ON BLACK

Hi Utsuri: This Koi has a black background with red (Hi) markings. The more solid the markings the better, although many have black spots caused by unstable Sumi.

Right: **Shiro Utsuri**
A striking mix of black and white.

Below: **Hi Utsuri**
Look for a bold colour contrast in this red on black Koi variety.

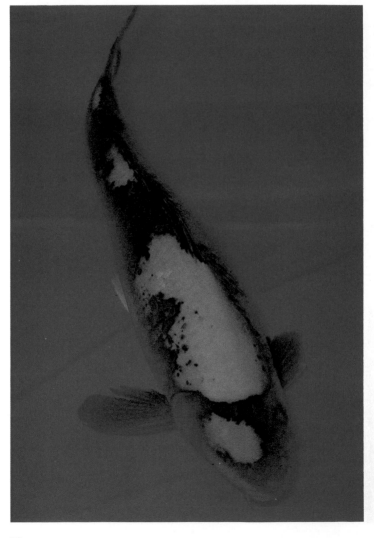

Above: **Asagi**
Matsuba scales in light blue.

Right: **Shusui**
The 'straight' form of this hybrid.

YELLOW ON BLACK

Ki Utsuri: This rare Koi is the yellow counterpart of Shiro Utsuri, i.e. with yellow markings on a black body. The yellow generally extends into the fins. Crossed with Ogons, the Ki Utsuri produces a range of spectacular metallic types called Kin Ki Utsuri (shown on page 100).

RED AND BLUE

Asagi: In this Koi – developed from the Asagi Magoi – the body is generally light blue with a pine cone effect on the scalation. The cheeks, abdomen and the joints of the fins are red. The lower part of the abdomen is milky white. Several subvarieties of Asagi have been developed, varying in colour depth.

Shusui: This is an Asagi crossed with a Doitsu fish. The head should be light blue and the back a slightly darker blue. The tip of the nose, cheeks, abdomen and the joints of the fins are bright red. The large Doitsu scales should be in neat lines, especially the ones that run down the middle of the back. The latter must be dark blue. Several Shusui varieties are recognized, including the following two:

Hana Shusui: This type has red markings on the areas of blue skin between the abdomen and the lateral line and between the lateral line and the prominent line of scales along the dorsal region.

Hi Shusui: Here, the red of the abdomen spreads upwards and completely covers the dorsal region, with the large blue dorsal scales still in evidence.

Above: Hi Shusui
*In this form of Shusui the red
completely covers the upper parts.*

Right: **Hana Shusui**
*Shusui pattern but with red between
dorsal scales and abdomen.*

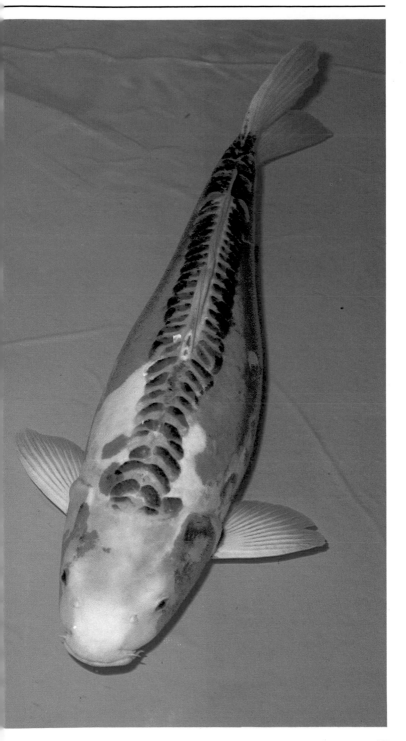

Above: **Kujaku**
A handsome colour variety of Koi that is basically a Yamabuki Hariwake or an Orenji Hariwake with a Matsuba (pine cone) overlay.

Right: **Hariwake**
The three types of Hariwake shown here are: Yamabuki (top); Doitsu (left); and Orenji (right). They are among the most elegant of Koi types.

METALLIC – VARIOUS COLOURS

Kinsui/Ginsui: Metallic Shusui. Those tinged in gold/red are called Kinsui and those with silver coloration are known as Ginsui.

Hariwake: This Koi has a predominately silver base colour with a gold pattern. There are many subvarieties of Hariwake with slight variations in coloration, including the following two:

Orenji Hariwake: A handsome fish in which orange-golden and platinum patterns predominate.

Yamabuki Hariwake: With patterns of bright golden yellow and platinum – an appealing combination.

Kujaku: A metallic Koi with Matsuba markings over a metallic yellow or orange and platinum base. (This and the following type are included with the Hariwake in the Hikarimoyo-mono Family.)

Kikusui: A beautiful fish of a platinum colour, which is particularly striking on the head and back. It has Doitsu scales along the rear of the dorsal region and irregular pale yellow markings on the body and in the fins.

Hikari-Utsurimono: Hybrids between Utsuri and Ogon families. Several two-colour varieties are available, including:

Ginshiro: A highly lustrous black on silvery platinum fish. This form is also known as Kinshiro Utsuri.

Kin Ki Utsuri: These metallic types of Ki Utsuri are very handsome Koi in black and yellow or black and orange. The former are hybrids of Ki Utsuri with Ogon and the latter are derived from crossings between Hi Utsuri and Ogon.

Below: **Ginshiro**
A fine blend of black and silver.

Below: **Kin Ki Utsuri**
An elegant Koi with a metallic glow.

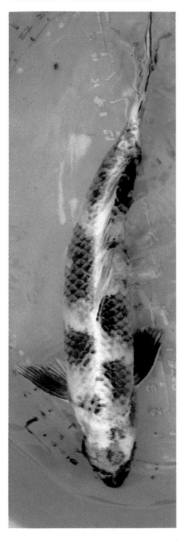

Kinginrin: Koi with numerous mother of pearl scales in either silver or gold, are designated as 'Kinginrin'. This can apply to all classes of Koi. In Kinginrin Kohaku, for example, the silver scales seen on the white portion of the Kohaku are called Ginrin, while those on the red portions are known as Kinrin. These iridescent scales can be given specific terms according to their size, texture and location.

Below: **Kinginrin Kohaku**
A Kohaku with glinting scales.

Koi colours and patterns	
Aka	Red
Beni	Orange-red
Cha	Brown
Gin	Silver metallic
Hi	Red
Ki	Yellow
Kin	Gold metallic
Matsuba	Pine cone pattern
Nezu	Grey
Shiro	White
Sumi	Black

Three-colour Koi

Above: A group photograph
featuring several three-colour forms
of Koi. As the following pages show,
these colour forms are principally in

the Sanke (or Sanshoku) group. The
colours involved are red, black and
white, although blue plays a part in
the coloration of Koromo hybrids.

Three-colour Koi are known as Sanshoku or, more generally, Sanke. The two main 'classes' featured here are Taisho Sanke and Showa Sanke. The colours involved are red, black and white, although in some types blue is involved.

Taisho Sanke: This koi has Hi (red) and Sumi (black) markings on a white background. Along with the Kohaku, these fish are held in the highest esteem at Japanese shows. Judging points would be the possession of a interesting Hi mark on the head while the Hi and Sumi of the main body pattern should be distinct and well balanced. As in the Kohaku, the white should be like snow. The overall appearance should be clear and bright. Cloudy skins and/or black specks on the white are not desirable. If the fish has black on the fins or gills, the body pattern has 'stabilized'.

Tancho Sanke: The red is restricted to a large round Hi pattern – representing the rising sun – on the head. There is no red on the body, which is white with Sumi markings.

Right: **Tancho Sanke**
A fine example of a popular type.

Below: **Taisho Sanke**
A universally favoured type of Koi.

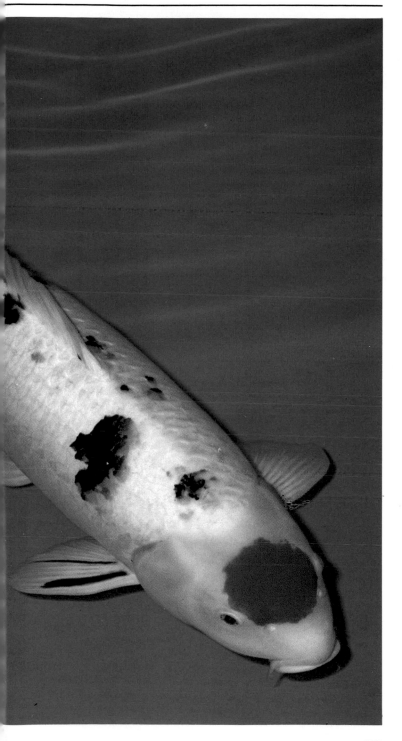

Aka Sanke: In this type the red extends from head to tail, and is overlaid with black markings.

Showa Sanke: Showa Sanke has a ground colour of black overlaid with red and white markings. As in other Koi, the colours must be clear with a distinct borderline. About twenty percent of white is desirable and this should be snow white. White markings must be present on the head, the joint of the tail and on the back. There should be a good-sized Hi mark on the head. The Sumi must be intense, forming a centrally placed lightning pattern on the back and extending over the sides of the fish and onto the abdomen.

Boke Showa: Here the Showa's back is in a netlike pattern.

Hi Showa: This fish has very little white and the Hi markings predominate on the back.

Kindai Showa: In this type the white predominates and the Sumi is relatively scarce compared with other Showas. This variety is very popular in Europe as well as Japan.

Above: **Kinginrin Showa**
A celebrated example of this Showa overlaid with a metallic sheen.

Left: **Kindai Showa**
In this form, the white is much more prominent and the black is sparse.

Right: **Hi Showa**
A striking form in which red is the dominant colour on the back.

Tancho Showa: Tancho Showa has no Hi on the body but has a Hi spot on the head.

Koromo: These hybrids of Asagi and Kohaku or Asagi and Sanke include the following four types:

Ai-Goromo: This is a cross between Asagi and Kohaku. Its Hi scales have distinctive blue borders.

Koromo-Sanke: This cross between Ai-Goromo and Taisho Sanke has blue shadows overlaying the Hi scales of a Taisho Sanke.

Budo Sanke: With blue/purple markings on the Hi.

Koromo-Showa: A cross between Ai-Goromo and Showa Sanke, with blue patches on the Hi patterns of the Showa Sanke.

Kin Showa/Gin Showa: Golden lustre specimens are Kin Showa; with a platinum lustre, Gin Showa.

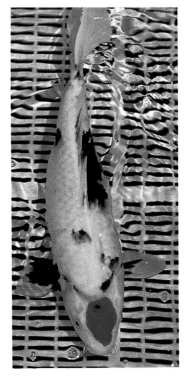

Left: **Tancho Showa**
Black can appear on the head area.

Above: **Koromo (Ai-Goromo)**
These hybrids of Asagi and Kohaku *are distinguished by blue patterning* *on the red (Hi) areas of the body.*

Above: **Ai-Goromo**
The blue borders of the red (Hi)
scales produce a characteristic
netlike body pattern in this form.

Above: **Kin Showa**
A Showa type of Koi with an

appealing gold metallic lustre
derived from the influence of Ogon.

Multicoloured Koi

With the numerous crosses between Koi groupings, there are many four-coloured fish and one, the famous Goshiki, has five colours: red, white, black, blue and dark blue.

Koi groupings
The Japanese have divided Koi into the following thirteen groups based on genealogy:

Below: **Goshiki** *Five-coloured Koi.*

1 Kohaku: Shiromuji, Akamuji (Higoi, Benigoi, Hiaka), Aka Hajiro, Kuchibeni Kohaku, Nidan Kohaku, Sandan Kohaku, Yodan Kohaku, Inazuma, Straight Hi, Doitsu Kohaku, Goten-zakura, Kinzakura

2 Taisho Sanke: Kuchibeni Sanke, Aka Sanke, Doitsu Sanke, Doitsu Aka Sanke

3 Showa Sanke: Boke Showa, Hi Showa, Kindai Showa, Doitsu Showa

4 Utsurimono: Shiro Utsuri, Ki Utsuri, Hi Utsuri, Utsuri Doitsu

5 Bekko: Shiro Bekko, Aka Bekko, Ki Bekko, Bekko Doitsu

6 Asagi/Shusui: Konjo Asagi, Narumi Asagi, Mizu Asagi, Asagi Sanke, Taki Asagi, Hana Shusui, Hi Shusui

7 Koromo: Ai-goromo, Sumi-goromo, Budo Sanke, Koromo Sanke, Koromo Showa

8 Kawarimono: Karasugoi, Hajiro, Suminagashi, Matsukawabake, Kumonryu, Kigoi, Chagoi, Midorigoi, Matsuba (Aka Matsuba, Shiro Matsuba), Goshiki, Sanke Shusui, Showa Shusui, Goshiki Shusui, Kanoko Kohaku, Kanoko Sanke, Kanoko Showa, Kage Utsuri (Kage Shiro Utsuri, Kage Hi Utsuri), Kage Showa

9 Ogon: Ogon, Nezu Ogon, Parrachina/Platinum Ogon, Yamabuki Ogon, Orenji Ogon, Hi Ogon, Kin Matsuba, Gin Matsuba, Doitsu Ogon, Parrachina Doitsu, Orenji Doitsu, Mizuho Ogon, Kin Kabuto, Gin Kabuto, Kinbo, Ginbo

10 Hikarimoyo-mono: Hariwake, Yamabuki Hariwake, Orenji Hariwake, Hariwake Matsuba, Hariwake Doitsu, Kikusui, Parrachina Kohaku, Yamatonishiki, Kinsui Ginsui, Kujaku Ogon, Kujaku Doitsu, Tora Ogon

11 Hikari-Utsurimono: Kin Showa, Gin Showa, Ginshiro (Kinshiro-Utsuri), Kin Ki Utsuri

12 Kinginrin: All kinds

13 Tancho: Tancho Kohaku, Tancho Sanke, Tancho Showa

Index

Page numbers in **bold** indicate major references. Page numbers in *italics* indicate captions to illustrations. Text entries are shown in normal type.

A

Acer sp. 35
Aeration systems 33
  air-exposure tower 33
  aquarium air pump 33
  mat aerator 33
  venturi tube *26, 28, 29, 32, 33,* ein2½33
Aeromonas sp. 64
  hydrophila **61**
Ai-Goromo **108**, *110*
Aka Bekko **90**
Aka Sanke **106**
Akame Kigoi 80, 83
Algae 52
Anacharis canadensis 42
Anatomy **12-13**
Anchor worm **58**, 68-9
Antibiotics 57, 68-9
Argulus foliaceus 62
  sp. **62**
Arrowhead 30
Arundinaria simonii 40
  A.(Sasa) veitchii 40
Asagi 74, 80, 83, *85, 94,* **95**, 108, 111, 113
Ascites **60**
Azalea 35, *40,* 40-1

B

Bamboo 35, 40
Bekko 113
Benigoi *79,* **80e**, *81*
Benzalkonium chloride 59, 61, 68-9
Boke Showa **106**
Bonsai 35, *40,* 41
Box 35, 41
Breeding **70-1**
Budo Sanke **108**
Buxus sp. 41
Buying Koi **44-7**

C

Canadian Pond Weed 42
Carp pox **58-9**, 68-9
Carassius auratus 11
  carassius 11
Chagoi *79,* 80, *80*
Cherry blossom 36
  tree 35
Chilodonella 64
Chloramine 61, 68-9
Cloudy eye **59**, 68-9
Columnaris **59**, 68-9
Common Carp 10, *13*
Costia 64
Crucian Carp 11
Cyprinus carpio 10

D

Dactylogyrus **63**, 64
Descriptive terms 76-7

Dimethyltrichlorohydroxyethyl phosphonate 58, 62, 68-9
Dipterex 58, 62, 68-9
Doitsu Goi 11
Dragonfly 67
Dropsy **60**, *63,* 64
Dylox 58, 68-9
Dytiscus marginalis 67, *67*

E

Eichhornia crassipes 30, 70
Exophthalmus **63**

F

Feeding routine 48
Filter designs **24-30**
  downflow *25*
  multichamber *26, 27*
  sand pressure 30, *31*
  undergravel 28-9, *28-9*
  upflow *24*
  vegetable 30, *30*
Filter media **22-3**
  baked clay granules 22, *23*
  Canterbury Spar 22, *23, 24,* 26, *26*
  filter brushes 23, *23, 24, 25, 26*
  foam 23
  gravel 22, *29,* 30
  plastic mouldings 23, *23*
  processed lava granules 22, *23*
  sand 22
    silica *31*
  zeolite 23, *23, 24,* 26, *27*
Filtration **22-31**
  biological 22-3, 28, 30, *30*
  chemical 22
  mechanical 22
Finrot **61**, 68-9
Fish leech **61**, 68-9
Fish lice **62**, 68-9
Flexibacter columnaris **59**
Fontinalis antipyretica 42
Foods
  bloodworms 50
  brineshrimp 71
  chlorella 51
  daphnia 50, 71
  duckweed 51
  earthworms 49-50, 52
  glassworms 50
  maggots 51
  mosquito larvae 50
  pelleted foods **48-9**
  Phantom larvae 50
  Spirulina platensis 49-50, 51
  tadpoles 51
  Tubifex worms 50
  water lice 51
Formalin 63, 64, 66, 68-9
Fungus **62**, 68-9

G

German Carp 11
Gill flukes **63**, 68-9
Gin Matsuba **83**
Ginshiro **100**

Gin Showa **108**
Ginsui **99**
Golden Orfe *14*
Goldfish 11
Goshiki **112**
Granite 36
Gravel 36, 38
Great Diving Beetle *67*, 67
Gyrodactylus **64**

H

'Hakuten' 66, 68-9
Hana Shusui **95**, *97*
Hariwake **98**
  Orenji **99**
  Yamabuki **99**
  Doitsu *98*
Hikarimoyo-mono 99, 113
Hikari-Utsurimono **100**, 113
Hi Matsuba **80**
Hi Showa 106
Hi Shusui **95**, *96*
Hi Utsuri*85*, **92**
'Hole disease' *65*
Hydra 67

I

Ich **66**, 68-9
Ichthyophthirius 66
Iris *35*, 35, 43
Iroage **51**

K

Kawarimono 113
Ki Bekko **92**
Kigoi *78-9*, **80**
Kikusui **100**
Ki Matsuba 80
Ki Utsuri **95**, 100
Kindai Showa **106**
Kinginrin **101**, 113
Kin Ki Utsuri 95, **100**
Kin Matsuba *82*, **83**
Kin Showa **108**, *111*
Kinsui **99**
Kohaku 10, 71, 74, 80, **86-91**, 108, 111, 113
  Goten-zakura **90**
  Inazuma *84*, **90**
  Kanoko **90**
  Kinginrin **101**
  Kinzakura **90**
  Kuchibeni **86**
  Makibara **90**
  Maruten **90**
  Nidan **86**
  Sandan **89**
  Tancho **86**, 90
  Yondan **89**
Koromo **108**, 113
Koromo Sanke **108**
Koromo Showa **108**
Kujaku *98*, **99**

L

Lagarosiphon sp. 42

Lernaea sp. **58**
Limestone 36

M

Malachite green 63, 64, 66, 68-9
Masoten 58, 68-9
Matsuba Ogon **83**
Mercurochrome 57, *57*, 58, 62, 68-9
Methylene blue 57, 68-9
Mirror Carp 10
Moss 36, 40
Mouth fungus 59, 68-9

N

Nezu Ogon 83
Nifurpirinol 59, 61, 68-9
Nymphaea alba 42
  'Colonel A.J. Welch' 42
  'Gladstoniana' *42*
  'Colossea' 42
  marliacea albida 42
  marliacea carnea 42
  marliacea chromatella 42
  'Moorei' 42
  'Masaniello' 42
  odorata alba 42
  tuberosa rosea 42
  'Attraction' 42
  'Charles de Meurville' 42
  'Conqueror' 42
  'Escarboucle' 42

O

Ogon *Endpapers*, 71, 74, *78*, *82*, **83**, 95, 113
Oodinium 59
Orenji Ogon **83**
Oxolinic acid 60, 66, 68-9

P

Parasites *58*, 62, 63, *63*, **64**, *65*, 66, 68-9
Parrachina *78-9*, **83**
Phenoxyethanol 59, 61, 68-9
'Pine-cone disease' 60, 68-9
Pines 35, 41
Piscicola geometra **61**
Pistia stratiotes 30
Ponds **14-21**
  concrete 16-7
  construction **16-21**
  design 15
  fibreglass 20-1
  flexible liners 18-9
  siting 14
  volume *17*
Pop-eye **63**, 68-9
Povidone-iodine *57*, 57, 68-9
Pseudomonas sp. 64
Predators 66-7
Pumps 31-2
  electrical consumption 32
  fittings 32
  fountain 31, 32
  output 32
  submersible *25*, *29*, 31
  surface mounted 31

waterfall 31, 32

Q
Quarantine 46

S
Sagittaria sp. 30
Salt 59, 60, 61, 63, 64, 66, 68-9
Sand 38
Sandstone 36
Sanshoku 104, 108
Saprolegnia sp. **62**
Septicaemia 64, 68-9
Shan Shui 34
Shiro Bekko *84*, **90**
Shiromuji **80**
Shiro Ogon **83**
Shiro Utsuri *85*, **92**, 95
Shishi odoshi *38*, 38
Showa Sanke 71, **106**, 111, 113
Showing Koi **72-3**
Shusui 74, **95**, 99, 113
Skin fluke **64**, 68-9
Skin papilloma *59*
Slate 37
Sliminess of the skin **64**, 68-9
Stratiotes aloides 43

Swimbladder trouble **64**, 68-9

T
Tailrot **61**, 68-9
Taisho Sanke 71, **104**, 111, 113
Tancho 113
  Tancho Sanke **104**
Tancho Showa **108**
Tapeworms **64**, *65*, 68-9
Transporting Koi 46-7
Trichodina sp. 64
Tsukubai 38
Tuffa rock 37

U
Ulcer disease **64**, *65*, 68-9
Utsurimono 113

W
Water gardens **34-43**
Water Hyacinth 30, 70
Water Lettuce 30
Water lilies *21*, 38, 42
Water Soldier 43
White spot **66**, 68-9
Willow Moss 42

Picture Credits

Artists
Copyright of the artwork illustrations on the pages following the artists' names is the property of Salamander Books Ltd.

Janos Marffy: 24, 25, 28, 29, 30, 31, 32
Clifford Meadway: 18-9, 20-1, 26, 27
Eric Tenney: 12-3, 76-7

Photographs
The publishers wish to thank the following photographers and agencies who have supplied photographs for this book. The photographs have been credited by page number and position on the page: (B)Bottom, (T)Top, (C)Centre, (BL)Bottom left etc.

Dr. Chris Andrews: 63(T)
Heather Angel/Biofotos: 10-11(Inset), 34-5, 35
Dr. James C. Chubb: 59(B), 61, 62(T), 64, 66
Eric Crichton: 39
Eric Crichton © Salamander Books Ltd: Title page, 18, 21, 23, 24, 29, 32, 33, 38, 46, 47, 48-9, 50-1, 56, 57
John Cuvelier: 43(T)
John Draper: Copyright page
Jerry Harpur: 36-7(T), 40-1(T)
Roger Hyde: 112-3
Ideas into Print: Half-title, 25(T), 45(T,B), 72-3, 74-5, 78-9(Inset)
Kent Koi Ko: Endpapers, 10-11, 44-5(B), 58, 60(B), 63(B) 65(C), 71, 78-9, 80-111 inclusive
Kent Koi Konstruction: 16, 17, 27(T),
Gregory Peck (BKKS): 43(B)
Nishikigoi Holdings: 65(T)
Laurence Perkins: 67(T,B)
Peter W. Scott: 14-5(B), 42, 59(T), 60(T), 62(B), 65(B), 70
Harry Smith Horticultural Photographic Collection: 37(B), 41(B)
Andrew Tovey: 14-5(T), 52-3

Acknowledgements
The publishers wish to thank the Kent Koi Ko for their valuable help in preparing this book. We would also like to thank Gregory Peck (British Koi Keeper's Society), Norcal Engineering Ltd., Peter W. Scott, Dr. Neville Carrington, and Karen Ramsay (for editorial assistance)

The superb gold of an Ogon